Liebe

One Man's Struggle to Survive in KZ Sachsenhausen, 1939–1945

Jerzy Pindera

Edited by Lynne Taylor

University Press of America,® Inc.
Dallas · Lanham · Boulder · New York · Oxford

Copyright © 2004 by
University Press of America,® Inc.
4501 Forbes Boulevard
Suite 200
Lanham, Maryland 20706
UPA Acquisitions Department (301) 459-3366

PO Box 317
Oxford
OX2 9RU, UK

All rights reserved
Printed in the United States of America
British Library Cataloging in Publication Information Available

Library of Congress Control Number: 2003117170
ISBN 0-7618-2834-6 (paperback : alk. ppr.)

♁™ The paper used in this publication meets the minimum
requirements of American National Standard for Information
Sciences—Permanence of Paper for Printed Library Materials,
ANSI Z39.48—1984

To my courageous mother,
Natalia-Lucja Oskiera

Contents

Foreword

Jerzy Pindera was raised in the small city of Chelm, then a part of the Austro-Hungarian Empire, on the eve of World War I. It would not remain so for long. The first decades of the twentieth century were a momentous time in that part of the world. The entire map of Central and Eastern Europe was dramatically redrawn, after the Austro-Hungarian Empire collapsed ignomiously at the war's end. Poland, which had not existed other than in hearts and minds since 1795, re-emerged from the detrius of the Empire at the negotiating tables of Paris peace negotiations. This new nation was just one amongst many, but one of the largest and potentially the strongest. It was a glorious opportunity to create something completely new from the remains of the old, to make real what had been a dream for too long. It had been over a century since Poland had last existed as a country, and times had changed dramatically. The new Poland was a tabula rasa, a chance for a grand political and social experiment. Poland chose to make a radical break with the past and to build a new republican democracy on the borders of the Soviet Union under the leadership of Josef Pilsudski. Pilsudski was a powerful figure in Poland, a near-mythical figure who, for many, embodied the new Poland - strong, socialist, ferociously dedicated to his new country.

The decade of the 1920s was a heady one in Poland, as the entire nation engaged in this enterprise of building a new country. It was not an easy task. Poland had been divided among no less than three empires, German, Russian and Austro-Hungarian, for over a century and melding together the three parts was proving a near-impossible challenge. Poland was also feeling threatened on all fronts by its new neighbours and throughout the 1920s, engaged in a series of border wars as it tried to expand and make firm its geographic definition. It

vii

was also not the most auspicious moment to try to build, as the global economy slid deeper and deeper into depression, dragging almost all, including Poland, with it. Unsurprisingly, Poland was deeply divided internally as everyone engaged in the debate about what Poland should look like and what Poland should be. By the late 1920s, there were ninety-two registered political parties in Poland, thirty-two of which sat in the national parliament. In spite of this, the future seemed to be boundless; the opportunities, endless; if only the right choices could be made. It was a heady time to be Polish.

For Jerzy Pindera, the world seemed his. His family was solidly middle class and well-established in Chelm. His mother was a teacher; his stepfather was a civil servant in the local government. Pindera enjoyed life, and there was much to enjoy. When he moved to Warsaw to attend the Warsaw Technical University and study aeronautical engineering, he threw himself into his studies, as well as student and city life. He was politically active, as well as involved in campus rowing, and he enjoyed an active social life. He took full advantage of the cultural life that flourished in Warsaw at this time. He joined the reserve forces of the military as a pilot. All of this changed suddenly when the Germans invaded in September 1939. Within days, he was mobilized, but almost as quickly, his army was defeated by the Germans on one side and the Soviets on the other. Poland was, once again, torn asunder, this time between the Germans and the Soviets. Within a year, he would be taken as a prisoner of war, escaped and then find himself arrested again as a fugitive and spy. His ultimate punishment - internment in a concentration camp outside of Berlin, KZ Sachsenhausen. This is the story of his imprisonment.

It is an unusual story on several counts. Jerzy Pindera was a Polish Catholic and a member of the Polish elite - a graduate student at university studying in a daring new field, at a time when very few went beyond even primary school; the son of well-to-do middle class parents; an officer in the Army's reserve forces; politically aware and involved. Unlike many Polish officers, however, he was only briefly interned by the Nazis as a prisoner of war. He escaped and was re-captured. This time, he was condemned to a concentration camp as a political prisoner, which gave him a very different, much less comfortable status. His sentence was "Return not desired". He was forbidden to work under a roof and he was to be worked to death. He entered the concentration camp Sachsenhausen as one of the lowest in the prisoner society, considered only marginally better than the Jews and Gypsies. His first two years in the camp were hellish and he came within weeks of dying from malnourishment, horrific overwork and abuse. Then the tides turned dramatically and he became a member of the prisoner elite, an engineer employed in the Construction Office or Baubüro of the camp. The story became a very different one at this point, as Pindera recovered his health, his spirits and more importantly seized the opportunities offered by his new-found position to both fight back and to protect fellow prisoners. The contrast between the two periods of his internment is stark, and highlights the complexity of concentration camp life. His story, then, gives us insight into one man's fight to survive and then, to turn the concentration camp system on itself. Finally, Sachsenhausen itself is revealed. This is a camp about which relatively little is known, as it was located in that part of Germany liberated by the Soviet Union at the end of the Second World War. While it is one of the lesser-studied camps, it was one of the largest and oldest. Pindera's story gives us two very different perspectives of the camp and its complex society, one from the bottom of the prisoner hierarchy and one from the top.

The work is an interweaving of what Jerzy Pindera called his "Fragments" - vignettes of his concentration camp experiences that he wrote many years later - as well as letters written to his mother from the camp, which she kept, and interviews conducted over the course of several months. The combination of recent memory with past recordings is a potent one, and revealing.

Part One

From Chelm to Sachsenhausen

In an interesting way, the story of Jerzy Pindera really begins with the story of Jozef Pilsudski. Pindera's family had strong links to Pilsudski - two of his uncles, as well as his stepfather, had fought against Russia under Pilsudski during the First World War, as officers in his First Brigade of the Polish Legion. Pilsudski, although a scion of an old Polish-Lithuanian noble family, was a staunch socialist and fought hard for Polish independence. Finally, in the aftermath of WWI, Poland was granted that independence and Pilsudski returned triumphantly to Warsaw to create a new Poland. Pilsudski had been a crucial part of the negotiations that led to the re-establishment of the country and was considered by many to have been its founding father. As Pindera explained, Pilsudski was enormously respected and loved by the majority of Polish citizens - his death in 1935 was deeply mourned by the vast majority of the population. Pilsudski was also Pindera's idol and role model.

The qualities of the man that caught Pindera's attention were manifold. In his numerous writings, according to Pindera, Pilsudski stressed patriotism, a strong sense of duty and an individual's obligation to society, a belief in social justice with a strong socialist bent to it, a firm belief in a democracy based on a strong notion of personal and political responsibility, as well as in a free market economy but one controlled by the state, in order to guard its interests, a notion of personal honour, and a good understanding of history and of politics. Pilsudski's sense of mission and purpose was evident when he said once: "When it was needed, I boarded the red street car. When the street car arrived at the stop called 'Independence', I stepped out".

As Pindera wrote...

Even the high school which I attended in the city of Chelm was under the strong influence of Pilsudski's followers. The curriculum

1

included, beside basics such as mathematics, physics and chemistry, also compulsory courses in introductory philosophy, physical education, religion and on contemporary political and social issues. The last subject required us to subscribe to three newspapers, which covered the political scene in the country between them. Pedagogically, the stress was put on the development of leadership abilities, responsibility and patriotism. During my school years I was very active in the Polish branch of the Scouting Organization and I also took some paramilitary courses. I graduated from high school in 1933 and passed the entrance examinations for the Technical University of Warsaw. At that time, every young man in Poland was required to serve one year in the military, so after graduating with a first degree in mechanical engineering in 1936, I decided to spend one year serving in the military. After that, I would be free to pursue graduate studies in aeronautical engineering.

As a university student, I was involved in two student organizations: the Academic Scouting Organization and, as a commandant in the Academic Detachment of the Riflemen Association, a paramilitary civilian association organized by Józef Pilsudski before World War One. I lived in the largest student house in Warsaw, in a room together with an American who became a good friend, Joseph Rutkowski from Dearborn, Michigan. From 1937 onward, I received a very comfortable government stipend which meant that I could enjoy much of what Warsaw had to offer. Of course, there were the obligatory lectures, laboratories and seminars, but there was also opera, operetta, theatre, good movies, good cafés, elegant dancing cafés, always opportunities to meet interesting and attractive young women with whom one could take walks in the beautiful King's Park in Warsaw, rowing sculls as a member of my University's rowing team and so on. It was a magical moment in time. In the summer of 1939, I also had six weeks of practical experience on the floor of an airplane factory in Warsaw, as this kind of practicuum was one of the conditions for graduation. I did not realize, of course, how useful this would be in the near future.

That August, I spent three weeks at the flying school in Tegoborze, refining my skills flying gliders. The University felt that good aeronautical engineers should know how to fly, thus all my expenses were paid by the government. The experience was as glorious as I had hoped. When in the air, I could see the river of Dunajec, where I had played as a young child. I was born in those mountains, in the small town of Czchów. It was all that a graduate student in aeronautical engineering could hope for. And yet, the situation was already tense internationally, and there was a frisson of tense anticipation. War was coming.

When Nazi Germany finally invaded Poland at dawn on 1 September 1939, Poland had been partially mobilized for war for months. She had already moved guns to the expected front on 23 March and 23 August of that same year, so that, when the Nazis invaded, full mobilization was quick. Nonetheless, the rout of the Polish forces was immediate and dramatic. Pindera mobilized immediately, as part of the general mobilization announced across Poland on 30 August 1939, and headed for Wlodawa, where his regiment, the Ninth Regiment of Heavy Artillery, was based. En route, he first stopped in Warsaw, to visit a dentist and pick up a few belongings from his room at the students' house. Then, still on the way to report, he stopped in Chelm to say goodbye to his family. As he explained, "When one goes to war, well, one is not likely to see one's family again." He reported to his regiment on 1 September 1939.

All the heavy artillery guns had been moved to the anticipated front already, taken by units which had been called up earlier, during the so-called "silent mobilization". Thus, when I reported for service, I was put in uniform and told to wait. That day, I was promoted to Second Lieutenant by the Supreme Commander of the Polish Army, along with every other reservist of my rank. I remember that the first bombs were dropped on Wlodawa that day and it was there that we learned some of the details of the invasion of the German army. We were in a difficult situation as we had no guns. All we had were rifles. So after a week, I believe, the order came that the people who had no guns should form a unit, an artillery unit called the Battery, and they should retreat east. I was appointed Deputy of the Commandant of this Battery. Even then, we did not have enough rifles. I believe I had only twenty soldiers who were actually armed with rifles and ammunition. And we had several dozen horses - heavy artillery horses. And so we began our retreat. Because of the indiscriminate bombing by German planes, we moved only at night. We stopped close to the city of Chelm which gave me an unexpected and welcome opportunity to see my mother, sister and stepfather again. It was on that visit that my stepfather gave me a pistol. It was, I believe, the same gun that he had

had when he served in Pilsudski's First Brigade of the Polish Legion during the First World War.

The next stop in our retreat was close to my military school in Wlodzimierz Wolynski. At that point, we were very short of money. So, I took a bicycle and rode there, where I reported to the Commandant of the school. I explained that I was in charge of this unit, but that we didn't have any money. So they gave me some. The region was already under German attack, and I saw some wounded soldiers as I returned to my unit. It was my first exposure to the results of war. One was ... a disturbing sight, because he had lost his jaw. That night, I slept in a farmer's barn; the night was illuminated by a burning village, a few kilometres away.

Then we retreated in the direction of Brzesc Litewski, along with thousands and thousands of other soldiers. It was very dangerous. A few airplanes could have devastated everything. We were moving very slowly, too slowly. Although I travelled in a car, in order to stay alert, our men moved on horseback. Travelling by horseback at night is very tiring, even at the best of times, for horses panic very easily and at night, everything looks strange. So we had to move cautiously, both for the horses' sake and also because of the war.

Near the city of Kowel, we lost the Commandant of the Battery. He told me that we should split the troops and that he would take a different route and that I should take the soldiers with arms and their horses and go ahead alone, without him. This was because we could move faster as a smaller unit. But he took the military kitchen with him, which meant I had a problem - how was I going to feed my men! Still, we separated. I was left with about two dozen armed soldiers and their horses, and we rode hard for Luck, a city in the east.

We arrived at Luck on 15 September. I stopped at a village close to the city and found accomodation for my soldiers. I then reported to the office of the Military Commandant of the city and they told me to wait for further orders. I told them about the rumours I had heard about a possible Soviet invasion and that I didn't want to wait, but my orders stayed the same. So I returned to my soldiers. The next day, I told them to stay put and not move, not even to show themselves outside of where they were resting, and especially not to show their weapons. You see, although the city was Polish, the villages were Ukrainian, or a mix of Ukrainian and Polish, and this could have been a problem. There was a long history of tension between the Ukrainians and the Poles, and the invasion seemed to have brought it to a boiling point.

So my troops stayed inside and I went to the city, out of uniform, to look around. I didn't like the situation because it was tense. I talked with some people. I spoke to the shopowners because they were a good source of gossip. The atmosphere in the city was very tense. As I walked around the city, I could not help but notice hundreds of cars, mostly of high quality, like Mercedes, abandoned in the side streets because of the lack of gasoline. Anticipating the invasion of the Red Army, I considered moving fast either to the south or west, to join one of the major units of the Polish Army. I knew that the NKVD, a precursor of the KGB, would consider me to be an enemy of the people, and I also knew that my name probably was on the Gestapo's list of those among the Polish intelligentsia and the Polish upper class to be exterminated. Taking one of the abandoned cars appeared to be one of my options, if I could find a truck big enough to accommodate my soldiers. The other choice was to acquire a small plane that I could fly out, if travel by car was impossible. So, I also checked the airfield and there I found two small Polish observation planes. In either case, it was necessary to find gasoline. At the railroad station I finally stumbled upon a large tank with beautiful high-octane gasoline, suitable for planes, so that problem was solved. All that I needed was to find a small barrel and a wheelbarrow and a wrench to open the valve of the cistern!

The next day, the morning of 17 September 1939, I returned to the city. The atmosphere in the city was even more tense, if that was possible. On the main street, I unexpectedly ran into a high school friend, Wladyslaw (Wladek) Jankowski, whom I had not seen for six years. He was very pale, and I asked him why. He answered that he had spent the last three years in a prison in the city of Lublin for illegal communist activities. The Communist Party of Poland was illegal at that time because, being a member of the Comintern, it was obligated to collect military, economic and technological information for the Soviet Union. Wladek was a communist and had been involved in a communist student organisation when enrolled at the Catholic University of Lublin. This meant, of course, that the youth branch became illegal, just as the parent party did, so he was put in jail.

Wladek was convinced that sooner or later the Soviet Union would have to enter Poland. He suggested that we both could go east together. He offered to protect me, saying that he would assure them that I was a decent man, and that no harm would be done to me. But I was in uniform; I was now an officer, a second lieutenant, as of 1 September.

So, it was impossible for me to go east to the USSR. I was in uniform!
So I declined. But we were old friends, so we did not part ways. I told
him that perhaps I would have to move west somehow, instead. He
promised to help me.

While we were talking, we could hear the sound of large engines
coming from the eastern part of the city. I believe all the city's
population was in the street. And then there appeared huge tanks,
HUGE! I had never seen such tanks before in my life! They were, I
believe, the TK14. They were huge tanks! Up to the ceiling! With
heavy guns, the calibre was at least 105mm - at least! Which is an
extremely heavy gun! With red flags waving and the tanks covered in
infantry soldiers. It was the Soviet army entering the city . The tanks
kept rolling past, tank after tank, rolling along the main street. Wladek
was overjoyed, but suppressed his enjoyment when he saw how
distressed I was. I was shocked. My world had crumbled around me.
The deadly enemy of Poland had invaded my country. For the first time
in my adult life, tears started to flow down my face. A scared young
woman standing at my left side touched my arm and asked what those
tanks meant and I was not able to speak. It was especially shocking
because we hadn't really expected Soviet troops. After all, we were
supposed to be fighting the Germans. It was incredible because there
was a non-aggression pact between Poland and the USSR. (*In August
1939, Hitler and Stalin had signed a non-aggression pact, promising
not to attack one another. Unbeknownst to the world, however, a secret
clause of the pact promised Stalin half of Poland if he did not react
hostilely to a German invasion and seizure of the western half.*) I told
Wladek that I had to do something, I could not give up.

There were rumours around that the Soviet Union came to help us
to defend ourselves against German aggression, but that could not be
believed. Leaflets dropped by the Soviet military planes shortly after
the demonstration of the might by the Soviet tanks clarified the
situation. I remember clearly two different leaflets. The first leaflet
stated that the "two greatest men in history", Josef Stalin and Adolf
Hitler, had decided to terminate the existence of the bourgeois Polish
State and the might of the powerful Polish landowners and to destroy
the apparatus of oppression of the Polish State. That meant all the
Polish administration was now illegal, all of the Polish police force was
illegal, all of the Polish military forces were illegal. The second leaflet
was in Ukrainian and encouraged the Ukrainians to rise up against
Poles, to destroy the Polish administration and to eliminate the Polish

population. A third leaflet was also dropped. It was the text of a speech given by the Soviet Prime Minister, W.M. Molotov, on 17 September 1939, written in Polish, but it was much less explicit than the first two leaflets. At that point, Wladek and I parted ways, but made an appointment to meet the next day.

The situation was clear – it was not possible for me to retreat with my soldiers toward the west. Those roads were already closed to us, because of the Nazi invasion, and the Soviet leaflets stated that I was now an armed outlaw if in territory controlled by the USSR. A bitter thought crossed my mind. Caught in a similar situation three hundred years earlier, during the Cossack uprising, a Polish aristrocrat Jeremi Wisniowiecki had managed to retreat westward, with his court and his army, from his headquarters in East Ukraine close to the Don river, by opening his route with sword and fire. But I was not Wisniowiecki and my two-dozen lightly armed soldiers were no match either for the Red Army units or for the well-armed Ukrainian guerillas. We would perish if we tried, although we also would perish if taken prisoners by the Red Army.

My assessment of the situation was confirmed that evening, when I was returning to my soldiers. It was already dark, so I felt safe - mistakenly, as it turned out. For at that moment, I ran into a Soviet patrol. Suddenly a powerful floodlight fixed on me. I was trapped. I heard the command, "Hands up!" Blinded by the light, I had no choice. The officer approached me and asked my rank. I told him, and he let me drop my hands. He was obviously 'regular army', not security. Security would not have let me do that. He demanded my gun, which I turned over to him. Then, to my astonishment, he told me to go! I hurried to my men, convinced that retreat westwards as a unit would be foolish in the extreme.

In addition, I was convinced that I was a threat to my soldiers, for I was a part of the "Polish apparatus of oppression", as the Soviet leaflets called it. So, I returned to my soldiers with a heavy heart to perform my final task as their commanding officer. Knowing the history of the Soviet Union and the methods introduced by Lenin and perfected by Stalin, I anticipated how my soldiers would be treated by the security apparatus of the Soviet Union. Thus, on my own authority, I released my soldiers from their duty, allowed them to exchange the horses, which were my responsibility, for civilian clothes and food and advised them to head west in small groups and to try to return to their homes where they could safely wait for orders. I told them that there was nothing I could do to help them and that they were not in much danger, but that I was in grave danger. That was why I could not go with them, as I would make it very dangerous for them. I spoke to the peasant farmer who was housing them and asked him if he would help them get civilian clothes, and he agreed to do so. I shook hands with my men and then left immediately. I spent the night in a building close to the airfield, as I didn't want to endanger my men with my presence, and everyone in the neighbourhood knew there was a Polish unit hiding on that farm.

The next day, 18 September, I was very busy. I left the village and met up with Wladek. True to his word and in spite of being a Communist and pro-USSR, he was still willing to help me. Together, we went to the railroad station, which fortunately was still not occupied by Soviet authorities, found a small barrel, a small wheelbarrow, as well as a wrench for the cistern, and filled the barrel with what proved to be good, high-octane airplane gasoline. So, picture it; the Communist Wladek Jankovski and the Polish Second Lieutenant Jerzy Pindera openly transported a barrel of gasoline in a wheelbarrow through the streets of a city now occupied by the Red Army, with the express purpose of helping me escape, and no one stopped us! In hindsight, it seems bizarre, but at the time our friendship overrode any political differences, so it all seemed very obvious. My duty, as I explained to Wladek, was to reach a fighting unit, so that I could continue to fight. Wladek, even though a Communist, respected my decision.

So we brought the gasoline to a schoolhouse at the outskirts of the airfield, where we stumbled upon two officers of the Polish Air Force and several, apparently wealthy, Polish civilians. It was clear that the officers would be the ones to have first priority, rather than the civilians. We also agreed that I had the strongest right to fly out and to choose which plane I would take, as I had brought the needed gasoline. We decided to take both planes, but the problem was that the planes were already under Soviet authority and were guarded by the Red Army. We thought that we could still, perhaps, steal them if we tried under the cover of darkness. After some debate, it was agreed that Captain Piotr Kamienski and I would fly one plane together (they were two-seaters) and we would head for Warsaw, where the Polish forces were still fighting. I believed that it was our duty to fly to Warsaw in order to report about the Soviet invasion and everyone agreed with me. I see now that it was nonsense, just bravado. But this was the way I was brought up and so it seemed right at the time, and so did everyone else, it seems. Wladek decided to stay with me until my departure, to help me as needed.

It was still dark when we rose. The airfield was enveloped in a fog which raised our spirits - the fog would make avoiding discovery that much easier. We could remember the location of the planes and so we found them easily, and filled them both with gasoline. We faced a momentary crisis, when we realized that the Polish signs on the planes were painted over – there were neither the red-white squares of Polish military planes, nor the signs "SP" used on the Polish civilian planes. This was a very serious problem. If we were shot down either by a Soviet plane or by a German plane, we would certainly be executed as spies in accordance with the accepted rules of war, because we were flying unidentified or unmarked planes. But we were pressed by the circumstances and when faced with choosing between the bad and worse, we chose the bad. I was supposed to fly with the Captain in the green plane, and the Lieutenant was supposed to fly the red one, with one of the civilians. But the green one did not want to start, only the red one started. And when it started, what a noise! And although there was still a fog, it was getting lighter. The sun was still under the horizon, but you could still see. So we had to make a decision quickly. The Captain decided that I would go with him in the red plane. The other officer was not eager to take the red one, because he figured he would have been a good target, with a plane of such a bright colour! But we wanted to fly, so we took it anyway. It was then that I finally said good-bye to Wladek. There you see it, a Communist, but he helped me escape his Army!

So we took off. With the noise of the engine, the Red Army knew something was happening and they were shooting at us, but with the fog, they could not see us to hit us. As we took off, I remember we just narrowly missed a huge radio tower. I remember the banners hanging on it, one for Poland and one for Ukraine. I felt that surely we were lucky, if we missed the radio tower! And then we broke through the clouds, into the wonderful warm sun! It was so peaceful! There was not a Soviet plane in sight. I fell asleep as we flew west.

I woke several hours later, when Kamienski told me that he did not know where we were and that the gasoline was almost gone. I looked around - the fog was gone, but so were the clouds, which made it very dangerous, as we were visible to everyone in the air and on the ground. We noticed a Polish farmer plowing a field and we landed nearby. He told us that the nearest city was Kazimierz nad Wisla, northeast of where we were. He thought that there were no Germany army units there, so we flew directly to the city, close to the ground, and with almost no gasoline left in our tank. We landed on the edge of a forest just outside of the city, covered the plane with tree branches to hide it, and settled in to wait.

Several minutes later, a man appeared. He asked us what we needed and we told him that we needed gasoline, and not necessarily high octane, and information about the Germans. He left for the city, telling us that he would take care of our needs. Half an hour later, a strange procession filed out of the city. Men, women, teenagers and children, bringing us gasoline, of all kinds, in whatever container they had - bottles, cans, anything. But it was gasoline! Interestingly, one of those people was a man by the name of Czeslaw Iberszer. I would meet him again, two years later, in the concentration camp.

Now that we had gasoline, we still had to decide where to go from there. The Captain was not sure whether it was safe to fly at all, let alone fly all the way to Warsaw. I convinced him that it would be still safer to fly, in spite of the colour of the plane. The locals had told us that there were no Germans between Góra Kalwaria and Warsaw, so it seemed safe. We took off about two hours before sunset, and flew low over the treetops, to make ourselves less of a target. Clouds had appeared again, creating a ceiling of about 100, 150 metres, and we did not have the navigation equipment for flying blind, which was another reason to fly low. Besides when one flies high, one is a target because one is more visible. We did meet one huge German bomber, but we must have seemed a peanut to them, as they did not bother with us. Still, he may have alerted the German anti-aircraft units, because we ran into heavy German fire when we flew above Góra Kalwaria. We thought that this must be a local German detachment, so we tried to cross the river to escape the fire, and continued north, but to no avail. We were trapped against the clouds, which had dropped to about 100 metres. We could see Warsaw, burning, just a few minutes' flying time away! We were flying in the centre of an eerily beautiful, if deadly, three-dimensional web of machine-gun and tracer fire. The tracer bullets each left a violet streak through the air, and exploded into a red rose of light. It was beautiful in a brutal, strange way, with the grey sky and burning Warsaw as a backdrop. Strangely, I don't recall feeling much fear of death, it seemed so obvious. I was much more concerned about getting mortally wounded, and dying slowly and painfully. So I crunched up, pulling my elbows into my sides, trying to make myself small. The plane was slowly being shredded by the hail of bullets - we could see the clouds through the holes in the wings above us, and the ground through the holes in the fuselage below us. At least the engine continued to work!

We had to get out of this trap quickly, however, which meant landing somewhere, but there was no place obvious. And then somebody was too good. I got hit in both my shins. There were six holes in my right boot, with three flesh wounds on the front of that shin. And on my left shin, there were more, with three holes in my left boot and one wound in my foot. At least they were only flesh wounds. I wiggled my toes, which moved, only they were wet. Oh well, I thought, as long as I can move my toes. And then, I don't know why, I looked up and I could see a black point or spot growing, coming straight at my face. Without thinking, I quickly put my hand in front of my face! Bomp! It exploded in the back of my hand, and I lost all feeling and use of it! It was a type of explosive bullet that had been banned by the Geneva Convention. Then Captain Kamienski exclaimed that he was hit in the foot and the bullet had exploded. It was nasty. Then the engine started to sputter and cough. It was time to land. Kamienski was a good pilot and, in spite of his wound, he got us down safely beside a forest. When the engine died, we could hear machine gun fire. Kamienski yelled, "Get out!", and dove out of the plane, to the ground and raced on his belly into a nearby ditch. I did not get out so easily. My right hand did not work and I could not remove my harness because of my hand, so it got tangled around my feet and I ended up hanging out of the plane upside down, with the sand being sprayed into my eyes, as the bullets hit the sand in front of my face! Fortunately the plane was between me, dangling, and the Germans, so I was shielded somewhat. After a few seconds - what seemed an eternity - I was able to free my legs and I fell to the ground. For some reason, the Germans chose to elevate their fire, and I could feel the bullets whizzing over my back and head as I wriggled into the ditch, keeping as close to the ground as possible. It seemed a moment of paradise, when I got into that ditch and out of the line of fire.

Eventually, the German patrol appeared. They were Wehrmacht, which turned out to be a lucky break, although I didn't really realize it immediately. One yelled, " Hands up!", and we complied. I was really furious - it was the second time in the last forty-eight hours that I had had to raise my hands in surrender to an enemy, first the Soviets, and then the Germans. It badly bruised my pride.

The commanding officer was a Lieutenant, young, slim, handsome and he had two duelling scars on his right cheek. It was common among German university students at the time, and was a sign of one's manhood, that one was gentleman, that one knew how defend one's honour. This gave me some hope. He ordered his soldiers to dress our wounds and asked us a question in German. I could not understand it because I had never studied German, so he asked one of his soldiers to act as a translator. To my surprise, this soldier spoke Polish, although a very ancient form of it - from the fourteenth or fifteenth century. It turned out that the unit was a part of the Eleventh Infantry Division and from East Prussia, which had once been a part of the medieval Polish Commonwealth.

His first questions were about our rank, whether we had any weapons, where we were coming from and where we were heading. He also asked why the plane had no markings. They were particularly suspicious of us because we were flying an unmarked plane, and they were not sure if we were really Polish officers. That would have had enormous implications for how they treated us, whether they considered us officers or not. I told him our ranks, explained that we had turned our weapons over to the Soviets already, and that we had acquired the plane at the airfield in Luck, which had been occupied by the Soviet Army. The Soviets had already painted over the Polish ensigna, I explained, and of course, we did not have time to repaint the planes before leaving. I expected to be treated as a spy, but evidently the officer believed us, because he chose to treat us as captured officers. I also explained that we were flying from Luck to Warsaw, to join the fighting. He laughed, and said we wouldn't be going to Warsaw as we were now in German hands. Meanwhile, the commanding officer gave an order, my boots were removed and the soldiers began to dress my legs. He told us that we were lucky. I looked at my right hand, which seemed ripe for amputation, and could see little lucky about the situation. He explained that, as an officer of the Wehrmacht, he believed in the old German code of honour among soldiers, and so would treat us accordingly, and provide us with medical care. However, two kilometres north of where we were was an SS division that ascribed to a different code and executed on the spot any captured Polish officers. And he repeated, "However, we are the Wehrmacht." In fact, within a few hours, I had proof of what he said, as I met several wounded Polish soldiers at the Wehrmacht's field hospital who had been stabbed with bayonets by SS soldiers after they had been taken prisoner and I saw no Polish officers at all. We had, indeed, been very lucky.

Meanwhile, the soldiers who had tended to our wounds then put us on soft straw and after a while, a carriage arrived, drawn by two horses, and with a driver and a doctor. It was a lovely carriage, with soft suspension, that they had 'requisitioned' from a merchant or landowner, very elegant and comfortable. The doctor, a major in the Wehrmacht, inspected our wounds, gave Kamienski an injection, and put us in the rear seat of the carriage. He climbed up beside the driver. By this time, the adrenalin rush of combat had worn off and we were in pain and our mood, gloomy. The doctor and driver took us to the field hospital, where we were checked again and registered. Each of us was given an indentity card to hang around our neck with a special category recorded on it, that of pilot. The hospital occupied a village school, the teacher's house and a church. I was assigned a place in the church, but I found the atmosphere inside oppressive, so in the middle of the night, I moved to the schoolhouse, put my coat under my head and tried to get some sleep.

The next afternoon, Captain Kamienski, who needed surgery, was transported to a regular hospital in Otwock and I was transported to a field hospital east of Warsaw, which was run by the Polish Red Cross and supervised by the Wehrmacht. There, I was put in a small room with three beds. The other two prisoner patients were also Polish officers, one from Warsaw and one from eastern Poland. The first one had a badly wounded upper arm; but fortunately for him it was the left arm and the bone was not destroyed. The second had a lighter wound - a deep flesh wound without much damage around it. It was not serious, just painful. However, the location of the wound was a source of serious embarrassment. He had been shot in the buttocks by machine gun fire, as he lay on the ground awaiting the order to attack. To be shot in the front was a sign of bravery; to be shot in the back, a sign of cowardice. To be shot in the buttocks - it was improper even to mention it!! So it was very humiliating whenever the dressing had to be changed, especially because all the nurses were young and attractive women. My most serious wound was my hand, which had swollen up to the size of a loaf of bread. I was very worried that I would lose it and the staff had already promised me that I would have a nice amputation. So, I was not very happy.

Then the door to the room opened and a young, blonde, attractive Red Cross nurse with shining hair entered. She looked at each of us, put her hands on her hips, and said only one word, "Cowards!" I was stunned. I was in pain and expected compassion or, at worst, sympathy, but instead we were accused of cowardice. At that time, it was the worst accusation one could level against a Polish man. All that I could reply was, "Why?" She explained that it was evident to her that we must have allowed the Germans to wound us because we were afraid of fighting on the battlefield. It took a long while to convince her that she was wrong.

Then an older German officer came in to check on us and, later that night, the doctor came to check to see if everything was in order. This kind of daily medical supervision seemed the norm in the German army. The doctor decided, at that time, that none of us needed immediate surgery. I began to hope that, perhaps, I would not lose my hand.

It was now 21 September, and I was moved to another, better equipped field hospital, also run by the Polish Red Cross, but under Wehrmacht supervision. This hospital was located in a luxurious villa in the garden city of Michalin, about twenty kilometres east of Warsaw. There were about 30 wounded Polish soldiers and prisoners there, as well as three Polish Red Cross nurses and one manager. On the third floor was a terrace, from which one had a clear view of Warsaw as it burned. In the evening, one could hear the constant roar of the heavy guns as they pounded Warsaw. I decided at that moment that I had to somehow escape.

A few days later, when the light wounds in my legs were no longer painful, a nurse took me to the general hospital in Otwock, about 10 kilometres away, to x-ray my hand. We had to walk into Otwock along the railway tracks, as that was the safest route. I learned that my hand was healing nicely, with no infection, and that the damage to the muscles and nerves was minimal, so that I would not lose my hand! It was wonderful news! I also saw Captain Kamienski there. He was doing all right, but was going to have to stay in the hospital a longer time. It turned out that his foot was badly damaged, but not badly enough to amputate. It only meant that he would not walk easily, which we agreed was not a bad price. He was very concerned about his wife who was living in Warsaw, and I offered to convey a message for him to his wife. Since I was planning to escape, I thought I might have an opportunity to deliver it. He gave me their address and then I returned with the nurse to Michalin.

On 28 September, Warsaw surrendered to the Germans and on 1 October, the German Army entered the city. Several days later, around 10 October, I decided it was safe to leave and head for Warsaw. As there were no guards at the hospital, I simply took some bread, filled my canteen, told the nurses to keep quiet and walked out of the hospital. I headed into Warsaw along the railway tracks. It was a long walk. I had no insignia on my coat - someone had lent me a black leather trenchcoat - and I put my military belt on my tunic under the coat and removed the insignia from my military field cap. About ten kilometres along, I saw an open bakery and bought a two-kilogramme loaf of rye bread. When I entered Warsaw from the east, it was through a neighbourhood called Praga. An old girlfriend lived there, Marysia, and I stopped in to see her. That part of Warsaw had not been damaged and there were many people on the street, including German soldiers, who were making friends with local girls. To my surprise, Marysia was home. She invited me in and served a large glass of good, strong tea and served it with a black cherry preserve, as I remember. It was delicious, and all very civilized and genteel. For just a moment, the war did not seem to exist.

After a short rest, I said good-bye to Marysia and left. It was a poignant moment, as I was determined to somehow continue fighting, and we both knew it was unlikely we would meet again. I crossed the Vistula River at the now-damaged Poniatowski Bridge and entered Warsaw proper. The scene was becoming the norm - many homes had been destroyed, there were piles of rubble in the streets, there were no streetcars, buses or even private carriages in the streets - all transportation had stopped. The pedestrians were mostly depressed, although a few young people were quite loud. And there were many German officers and soldiers in the streets.

I went to the Women's Academic Residence on 6th August Street, which was very close to my University and where another girlfriend lived. There, I learned that the student residence where I had lived now was occupied by the German army and that everyone from there had moved into another Women's Academic House on 4th Tamka. So I went there and was assigned a small single room and given a large ration of marmelade. At least my basic needs were taken care of - a roof over my head and food for several days.

The next day I went to the Polish military hospital for officers, at Aleje Ujazdowskie, to try to get some information about what was happening. The news was not encouraging. The Polish military and civilian authorities were not recognized by the German authorities. The Polish Army in Warsaw had surrendered only as the Polish army in Warsaw, without contact with or permission from the Polish Supreme Command, which compromised the army's position. Everyone expected the German military commander for occupied Poland to order all Polish officers to report to a camp for prisoners of war. I was advised to abandon my uniform quickly, because it soon would be dangerous – my bandaged hand and the bullet holes in my boots would only offer limited protection. I was told I could stay at the hospital, but I found the atmosphere was too depressing, so I left.

I realized that I was very close to the neighbourhood in which Piotr Kamienski lived, so I went in search of his wife. When I knocked on the door, she was the one who opened it. When I told her that I brought news about her husband, she turned pale and was speechless, so I hastened to add that he was in the hospital in Otwock and that his wound was not life-threatening. She was so happy that she embraced me and kissed my cheeks, with tears in her eyes.

From there it was a long walk to my old student residence. It was risky, because it was now a headquarters for the German Military Police, but all my belongings were there and I needed them. Of course, the guards at the entrance to the building stopped me. They demanded that I identify myself, so I showed them my military book, the new identity card issued at the military hospital and my identification card as an inhabitant of that building. Somehow, in spite of not having a common language (at that point, I spoke very little German), I finally persuaded them that I just wished to take some of my belongings most important to me. To my surprise and relief, they actually let me into the building, without a guard, although they made it clear it would only happen once. They also told me that I did not need a key, because all the doors were open. It was soon clear why they were so free with me.

My room was in the side wing of the building, on the ground floor. I entered my room and froze – the room had been looted, and not by the Germans. Everything of value was gone. Only pages, torn from a leather-bound photo album, were left, scattered on the floor. I developed a bitter taste in my mouth. So, while some were fighting, others were looting. It made me think of a line from Hamlet, " For some must watch while some must sleep/ So runs the world away." I picked up the photographs and looked around, trying to remember the spirit of this place when I was just a student contentedly finishing his master's degree, and then left. The situation was becoming serious. I had no civilian clothes, I was wounded, I was not sure when my hand would be of use to me, and I had very little money. I knew that it would be dangerous to walk about in a Polish uniform, but I had no choice. Fortunately, at least for now, many young men were in military uniform, although without insignia so, for now, I did not stand out. Still, I returned to Tamka Street with a heavy heart.

It was already getting cold that autumn, and my room was poorly heated because of the lack of fuel, so I decided to try to rig a sort of electric heat. I learned that there was an electric shop in Nalewki Street. That street was in the Jewish quarter, but at that time it still was relatively safe to go there. The shop owner was an old, tall, very pleasant Jew. He charged me the regular price, which was exceptional, given the already thriving black market. I felt pity for him and suggested that, when the railroad transportation was restored, he should attempt to take the train east and cross the river Bug. In this way he would leave the part of Poland occupied by the Third Reich and enter the eastern part of Poland occupied by the Soviet Union where he would be safe. Life was already dangerous for Jews, who were getting singled out by the Germans for especially demeaning tasks and harsh treatment. He told me that the Jews had learned how to survive over the millenia. He felt that his money could buy him security. He did not believe me that Adolf Hitler was any different or more ruthless than Genghis Khan or Tamerlane. His answer was: "We will manage. In the worst case, we will lose all our money."

In late October, the German Military Commander for Occupied Poland announced, via very large posters, that all mobilized reserve officers of the Polish army should report to specified assembly points, from which they would be transported to prisoner-of-war camps. Any Polish officer who failed to obey that order would be executed. That order changed the situation dramatically and instantly. I was sure that the Gestapo would check the curriculum vitae of all the officers in the camps and that my name would be marked, because I was one of the commanders of the University of Warsaw's Academic Detachment of the Zwiazek Strzelecki, a liberal paramilitary organisation. It was an organisation strongly opposed to the growing fascist movement in Poland. I knew I would be in great danger if I turned myself into the Germans. Yet, I was in uniform and too visible; I had to do something about it. In an effort to gain some legitimacy, I registered in the National Socialist Welfare Register, (one had to register there in order to receive any benefits, such as rations) and received an identity card numbered 1529, stating that I lived in Warsaw at Tamka Street, No. 4.

Fortunately, at that same time, it became possible again for Poles to travel - a ban on circulation that the Germans had imposed was now lifted. There was no train service to Chelm at that time, so I borrowed a bicycle from one of my colleagues, obtained a pass to travel to my home, and started the 250-kilometre-long trip, via the city of Lublin. When I arrived several days later, I found my mother and sister, Danuta or Dani, in our apartment, but my stepfather was gone. My stepfather had been a government official at the county level in the Polish government. He was also in the Polish Security Division, which had been responsible for dealing with German and Ukrainian underground activities in the area. This meant that he was in grave danger. He was trying to cross into Roumania on foot, but he must have been too slow, because we heard a rumour that he only made it to the city of Lwow. Only later did we learn that he was arrested by the KGB and deported to one of the infamous camps in Komyla where he ultimately perished.

As I had no civilian clothes and no money to buy any, my mother dyed my military uniform black, which made it less military-looking, and less conspicuous. The most immediate and critical problem at that moment was trying to find a way for my mother and sister to support themselves. My mother did have some resources. The Polish government had foreseen the war and all the employees of the Polish state received a double paycheque in August 1939. The Polish government took care of its people, but it was still not much. The black market was already thriving and the price of food was rising rapidly. To make things worse, the elementary school where my mother had been teaching was closed because the majority of pupils were Jewish, so my mother's salary had stopped.

I had already decided that I could not stay in Chelm. I had heard about a clandestine order commanding all Polish officers to escape to the Polish Army in France, if possible. More ominously, the Gestapo were getting more aggressive. I remember one day in November 1939, when my mother returned from the city with the news that Gestapo was looking for young men. So my mother put me to bed and put a sign on the door with the word "Typhus.". It was well known that the German authorities were very reluctant to risk exposure to such infectious diseases, so this gave me some temporary protection. That November, there was also a persistent rumour that the Gestapo had arrested all the professors of the oldest university in Poland, the Jagellonian University in Kraków, as well as many professors from the Akademia Górnicza in Kraków. All of those university professors were sent to the concentration camp Sachsenhausen in Germany, according to the rumour. We knew about this camp. It had been established in 1936 and had been mentioned in the Polish press even before the war. So, the word "Sachsenhausen" was already ominous in Poland and the incredible arrest of the professors of one of the oldest universities in Europe added to its evil meaning. This, combined with the rumour that some units of the Gestapo and SS had started executing Polish intelligentsia en masse in the western part of Poland incorporated into Third Reich, made it apparent that I had to leave Poland quickly.

But at first I had to take care of my family. At first I tried to sell cigarette paper used to roll cigarettes by hand. I bought the paper very cheaply, but didn't realize the significance of the watermarks on the paper. They were in Russian, as the paper had been manufactured for export to the USSR. It was not a very successful venture. I was not a salesman and they did not sell well. In fact I was very embarrassed, because trade was held in low regard in traditional Polish society. I decided to try selling the paper in the east, along the demarcation line between the German- and Soviet-occupied territories, so I took the train east, in the direction of the river Bug.

I did not know how to approach potential buyers and so I did not sell a single cigarette paper booklet. However, when walking through one village, I managed to attract the attention of a Gestapo agent and was arrested. He was certain that I had crossed from the Soviet-occupied Poland illegally, because of the Russian language watermark. It took a very long time to convince the Gestapo agents that the cigarette paper was fabricated in Kraków and was meant to be exported to the Soviet Union. I was finally released with a serious warning not to return to the border region.

The next enterprise that I tried was smuggling tobacco leaves from Lublin province to Warsaw. However, it was very risky, and not very profitable, so I soon quit. Instead, I decided the right strategy would be to produce something that was in short supply. Looking around I realized that soap was in very short supply. I had taken a good course in chemistry so I taught myself how to make soap. I perused my chemistry books and figured out that I needed colophony, fat, caustic soda and salt. Salt was easy to buy, as was a low grade beef fat. I bought colophony in a National Forest not far from Chelm, but I had to travel to the factory in Kraków to get the caustic soda. When I got there, I

found out that it was sold in fifty kilogramme barrels! It was quite a
trip, coming home. All along the way, others were very helpful, helping
me lift it in and out of the train carriages (I had to change trains twice,
as well as get the barrel to the train in the first place). In one of the
stations, a Wehrmacht soldier even helped me! It took me two weeks to
learn how to make soap, but afterward I started to make money, selling
the soap on the black market, and my family became as financially
secure as one could be in those times. By then it was Christmas Eve,
and we had reason to celebrate - although it was hard without my
stepfather.

In spite of the improved financial security, our situation was
precarious. It did not help that my mother also did not believe in giving
in to the Germans. Our apartment was above the printing shop of the
weekly *Zwierciadlo* or *Mirror*. The *Mirror* was confiscated by the
Wehrmacht and converted into a German propaganda weekly. They
also confiscated one room in our apartment, which had a separate
entrance, for the weekly's editor-in-chief. He was a typical middle
class, educated German, with a master's degree in history, I believe, but
with the rank of an enlisted man. His behavior was correct. As he liked
playing music, he often came to our part of the apartment to play the
piano.

One evening the German knocked on the connecting door and,
when my mother bade him come in, he entered carrying a letter in his
hand. The letter was in Polish, was addressed to the editor of the
Mirror and he wanted my mother to translate it into German. My
mother could read German because she was born in the Austrian part of
Poland and was a subject of the former Austro-Hungarian Empire. My
mother started to read it aloud and I was shocked. A Polish peasant was
denouncing his neighbor, accusing him of anti-German activities.
Unbelievable. My mother looked at the editor, said that this was a very
bad letter and tore it into small pieces and threw it into the garbage can.
I froze, horrified at what she had done. The editor was clearly surprised
by her precipitous action, but very quickly recovered, smiled slightly,
and said simply, "All right." He then turned and left. I started to breath
again.

This was not the only time my mother challenged German
authority. By Christmas, the rumours were flying that a drastic action
against the Jews was coming soon. Some Jews, including a young
female friend of my mother's, decided to escape to the Soviet
occupation zone, across the River Bug twenty kilometres away. There

were consistent rumours that Jews were well received there, and certainly safer than in the German-occupied territory. The biggest problem facing these people was how to get out of the city and to the border. Jews were restricted from travelling and already any Poles who helped Jews escape were punished by immediate execution. However, once there, it was simple to get across the demarcation line - the Soviet troops apparently welcomed the Jewish refugees. One snowy evening that December, my mother asked me to help her assist her friend in escaping. In spite of the heavy risk involved, I agreed.

Early the next evening, after dark had fallen, my mother and I hired a horse-driven carriage and told the driver that we would be picking up one more passenger. I suspect the driver understood what we were doing, because he briefly hesitated, but finally nodded his head without a word. We met my mother's friend on a side street and she climbed into the carriage, carrying one small suitcase. She wanted us to take the poorly lit sidestreets, but I told the driver to take the main street, which we did. My mother and I rode in the back seat of the carriage, facing the driver where we were more visible. The friend rode behind the driver and thus was less visible. The street was full of German officers, Wehrmacht and Gestapo, relaxed and smiling, showing that they were the masters. I expected this and believed that that no German officer would suspect that somebody would dare to do something illegal so openly. And it worked, as we really did not attract undue attention! However, it was a very tense ride - made worse by the fact that we had to pretend to be smiling and relaxed. We delivered my mother's friend to her destination safely and returned without speaking. That evening is engraved in my memory.

During my travels, I had heard various rumours about resistance organisations, and about a Polish Army re-forming in France. In the city of Kielce, I also heard about Kubal, a Polish major and commander of a cavalry group who had refused to surrender and was waging a local partisan war against the Germans, hiding in the dense forests of the region. I also had heard that the Polish authorities had organized several 'underground railroads' to smuggle Polish officers out of Poland and into Hungary. Apparently in Budapest, there was an unofficial Polish office that was helping Polish refugees. Then the rumours of the mass execution of large numbers of the Polish population and the extermination of the Polish intelligensia became more certain. My decision became obvious - I had to get to France via Hungary and fulfil my military duty.

I approached two of my university friends, asking them if they wanted to flee to Hungary with me. At that time, I had managed to borrow a black leather trenchcoat from a friend to replace my more obviously military-cut coat. In February 1940, I returned to Warsaw to arrange the trip. I was wearing my now black uniform, artillery boots, complete with holes, and carrying my military haversack with some personal items in it and about 300 zloty (the Polish currency), as well as my military book and the German-issued identity card, as proof that I had fulfilled my military duties. We decided that we would do without a guide (I was afraid that the underground organisations might have been infiltrated by the Gestapo already), but just in case, I got the address of some people in the city of Sanok who were part of the underground railroad. We soon left Warsaw, travelling to Krakow, then Tarnow, and then to Stroze, Jaslo i Krosno. We finally got off at a place called Miejsce Piastowe, near the Hungarian border.

From there, it was dangerous to continue to travel by train - the border was densely patrolled. In fact, even changing trains could be dangerous. In one of the railroad stations, I noticed several German police officers checking the documents of passengers. I looked around and noticed a young Luftwaffe officer who was drinking vodka at the bar. So, I took a place next to him at the bar and took out from my breast pocket a hip flask filled with 75 percent proof vodka. I offered him a drink and he became talkative and friendly. He was a bomber pilot and I had to listen to how he had bombed Warsaw, but it was a small price for the security that he provided. No German police officer asked me to show my documents. So we set out on foot from Miejsce Piastowe, in the direction of the town of Dukla. The snow was about one metre deep, and the temperature well below freezing, so by the time we reached Dukla, we were tired and cold. Since we didn't know anyone in the town, we sought out the schoolmaster, who was very friendly, but who warned us that we could not cross the border there - the snow was too deep and the German guards were too alert. He put us up for the night, and then we returned to Miejsce Piastowe. By this time, my companions were discouraged and losing interest. They were in a very different situation than I was - they had not been in the army, nor had they belonged to any organisation that was considered hostile by the Nazis. Unlike myself, they had a good chance of surviving the German occupation. We decided to part ways.

As I was alone, I decided to go to the city of Sanok, contact the underground organization, be assigned a guide and a route and follow instructions. I did not like it because the organization could already have been penetrated by the Gestapo, but I had no choice. I do not remember much of that train trip, but I remember some parts vividly. I remember traveling at night in a carriage full of people active in the black market. "Full" meant an eight-person compartment with sixteen people crammed in. Of course, fortunately, no ticket control was possible in such conditions. I also remember a large railroad station where I had to change trains. It was early in the evening, but the sky was already dark. When I left the warm restaurant to board the train, I noticed that the German police were checking the documents of the passengers before allowing them to enter the train. I thought about returning to the restaurant, but the German officials were already at the entrance, checking tickets and documents. I looked for rail carriages reserved for the Germans and noticed that one carriage was evidently reserved for the German military, because only SS soldiers entered it. Having nothing to lose, I straightened my back, lifted my chin, pulled my cap deeper over my eyes, and entered it. It was dark, my clothing was black , with a military cut. The holes in my boots perversely reinforced the military image. I took a place at a window, pulled down my cap and pretended to go to sleep. I fit right in, as everyone on the car was sleeping - and there was no conductor, nobody checking tickets or documents - so it worked; nobody bothered me!

I do not remember how I found the safe house in Sanok, but I vaguely remember the apartment. It was a typical apartment of a member of a small city's working intelligentsia. I remember the young woman who ran the safe house. She was blonde, pretty and attractive, in her early twenties. That young woman assured me that the guide was reliable and that I would be safely guided to the Hungarian side of the border. She gave me the name of the guide – it was Bryndza, living in the village Szczawne-Kulaszne, where there was a short stop for the commuter trains. To my recollection, she did not know the location of the guide's house, but assured me that everybody in Szczawne-Kulaszne could give me his address. I did not like it but, somehow, I failed to draw the obvious conclusions. My cover was that I came to buy pepper in Hungary, but it was a very transparent cover, because I carried with me my military book and my German identity card in which I was identified as an airman. It was not very healthy to carry such documents in the border region.

Late in the afternoon of 14 February 1940, I boarded a train going in the direction of the city of Lupków. On the train, I met a man who told me that he knew where to find accommodation for a night at Szczawne-Kulaszne because he was going to that village as well. By the time the train arrived, it was already dark. As soon as the train had stopped, it was surrounded by the Gestapo's Ukrainian division (the Ukrainische Hilfspolizei), who checked the documents of all passengers leaving the train. There was only one solution for me – to be bold. So, I switched on my flashlight, holding it in my left hand, directed the light beam into the eyes of the Ukrainian policemen and waved my right hand horizontally – an international sign demanding a free passage. It worked and I and my companion were able to leave the train unmolested.

We walked a few hundred metres down the village street, in total darkness, to a cottage where my companion was known and where we were allowed to sleep on the floor. At least it was warm and dry! When he learned that I wished to go to Hungary to buy pepper, my companion offered to guide me through the mountains across the Polish-Hungarian border, but I did not trust him and I declined his offer. Then I made a mistake. I failed to ask our host, who was very friendly, for the location of the cottage of Mr. Bryndza. That failure was fatal, as I realized a few hours later.

Early in the next morning, I said good-bye to both my companion and to my host. The day was beautiful, with a clear sky. However, things went terribly wrong that day. I don't know why I did what I did, it was as if I was an automaton. I went to the railroad station and asked an employee there where Mr. Bryndza lived. I knew that this was wrong because such a direct question was dangerous, but I went anyway. He pointed out Mr. Bryndza's cottage, a few hundred metres away from the other cottages, and I walked over to the cottage, knowing that I should have asked whether Mr. Bryndza was at home. I walked slowly because the snow was high, at least half a metre thick. I did not even check whether I was being followed. I walked like an automaton.

I knocked at the door of the cottage and was admitted by a young woman. She told me that Mr. Bryndza was not at home. When I inquired when I could see him, she replied that he had been arrested by the Gestapo three days ago. Something was obviously very wrong with the Polish underground organization in Sanok – I should never have been sent to a guide who had already been arrested. At that moment, two armed Ukrainian police soldiers entered the cottage and told me to raise my hands. That was too much for me. Twice, being forced to put my hands up, once to the Soviets and once to the Germans. I became angry and my personal safety became irrelevant to me. I replied angrily that I was not armed, so I did not need to raise my hands, and I kept my arms down. Strangely, we were speaking Polish, nor were they particularly hostile. Apparently, they were just performing a task assigned to them by the Gestapo.

The Ukrainians took me back to the railroad station. After a while, I was told that I would be taken to the village of Komancza and to their local headquarters. Shortly afterwards, I was put in a horse-drawn sled, with one armed guard. In different circumstances that trip, about two hours long through fields and woods covered heavily by snow, would have been wonderful - it was a bright February sun, there were no clouds and the snow sparkled – but my mood was heavy. True, I considered the fact that I was strong, stronger than my guard, so I could have overpowered him easily, then overwhelmed the driver and escaped. However, inexplicably, I had lost my will to fight. I have never understood what happened to me at that moment. It was not fear. I just lost my will to fight. My guard was not unfriendly and we chatted a bit. I mentioned that I had come to the border region to buy pepper; clearly he did not believe it, but he strongly indicated that I should keep to my story.

In Komancza, I was briefly interrogated by the chief commanding officer. He made me wait in his main office. The office was decorated with a number of nationalistic Ukrainian posters and I started to read them aloud. The commander asked me where I had learned Ukrainian and his attitude became almost friendly. He asked me to hand over all my documents and to explain why I had come to Szczawne-Kulaszne. With all my documents and my notebook with the addresses of the Polish contacts in Budapest spread out on the table, I knew my story about buying pepper would not work. I was afraid that if I insisted on that story, and then he read the documents and learned the truth through them, the results would be disastrous. So I admitted that I was trying to escape to Hungary. Maybe I was too cautious and maybe I should have taken the risk. I remember that the friendly Ukrainian guard who transported me from Szczawne-Kulaszne to Komancza stared intensely at me, as if he wanted me to deny my intent to cross the border. But simply and inexcusably, I had lost my will to fight.

With my admission, the Ukrainian officer relaxed. He spoke Polish well, so we conversed in that language. He told me that he was a Polish citizen of Ukrainian descent. After having graduated from a Polish high school, he went illegally to the Third Reich to obtain a military education, with the hope of being one of the future leaders of the Ukrainian Uprising Army in Poland. He returned to occupied Poland with the SS and had been appointed the commander of this detachment of the Ukrainian police, under the control of the Gestapo. He said that my knowledge of the Ukrainian language impressed him and that he did not think that I was hostile to the Ukrainians. He was surprised that I even knew a few lines of the Ukrainian national anthem! Given all of this, he told me that he was going to make an exception – I would be delivered to the Gestapo in Sanok alive and in good health. Evidently, I made some kind of impression, because he added that I was the first Laszek to be delivered to the Gestapo not only alive, but also without any injury. (Laszek is a derogatory Ukrainian term derived from the medieval term Lach, or Pole). Normally, I should have had belts drawn from the skin on my back, a medieval punishment common in that part of Europe, but he would make an exception in my case. Perhaps he was joking, but I took it seriously at that time. My impression was that he would have released me if he could have. He was certainly not a National Socialist. I suspect that the Third Reich intelligence services had promised him and his friends that they would get to establish a free Ukraine under the protection of the Third Reich. That night, I was delivered to the head of Gestapo in Sanok and put in prison. The prison administration was still Polish, so I was not treated harshly. I had to hand over my documents and my military haversack, containing all my belongings. The head of the prison told me that he was putting me into the cell with other Polish political prisoners.

I crossed the threshold of the cell and looked around. This was evidently an old prison and it had very high ceilings – at least four metres high. The cell was rather small for eight or ten prisoners and looked uncomfortable. The floor of the cell was made of wood. There was one window opposite the door, high and covered on the outside by boards, so only a small piece of the sky could be seen. In one corner, there was a pile of straw mattresses and simple cotton blankets. In the opposite corner, close to the door there was a large, simple steel barrel with two handles and a wooden cover with a handle. Evidently that barrel served as a makeshift toilet. Close to it, there was a hand basin on a wooden stool and a simple steel jug for washing water. In the middle of the cell, a wooden table with several wooden chairs was located. There were about ten prisoners living in that cell and they all turned to looked at me.

It was, of course, the first time I had ever been in a prison, certainly the first time I had been a prisoner. I had no idea how to behave in such a situation, what to do, so I stayed standing at the door. One of the prisoners approached me and very formally, introduced himself. He was a public prosecutor from the city of Plock. He asked for my name and my own social position. Now I was on a solid ground. I stated my name and briefly described my background as a student and a mobilized reserve officer. I did not state the reason for my imprisonment, nor did anyone ask. The prosecutor introduced me to the other prisoners. They were mostly from the intelligentsia – besides the public prosecutor, there was a judge from the city of Bochnia, a teacher from the city of Brzesko, a surgeon who had been serving in the Polish Army at the rank of a major, and a catholic priest. Sadly, I have now forgotten all their names. At least they proved to be good company! I was assigned a place for my mattress and told how to use the toilet. This proved quite difficult to get accustomed to. Also, the unofficial daily routine was explained – namely, every morning a different prisoner had to state how many days were left until the end of the war. As I remember, at that time, we believed the number of days to the final victory of the Allies was expected to be about two hundred days – quite an understatement, as I learned over the course of the next two thousand.

I learned the prison routine quite quickly – reveille, stating how many days were left until the end of the war, collecting and piling in a corner the mattresses and the blankets, washing, carrying out the full toilet, breakfast, dinner, supper, washing, laying out the mattresses and sleep. The food was sufficient and tasty. The prison administration was polite and as obliging as possible. Once a week, each cell was allowed to exercise in the prison yard, although it was for no more than half an hour. I believe that once every one or two weeks, each cell was taken to a shower room, as well. Of course, no letters, newspapers or books were allowed – we were completely isolated from the outside. When a prisoner needed dental care, he was escorted to a dentist. When he was not feeling well, he was allowed to lie down on his mattress – no questions asked. I remember that I lay down several times when I was depressed. To distract myself, I would make myself solve differential equations or by derive formulas of differential geometry in my head. Of course, writing material was off limits to us. Nevertheless, on some occasions, it was possible to smuggle some items into the cell. This was not always to our advantage. I remember, one day, a page of the

Warsaw newspaper, *Nowy Kurier Warszawski* – a newspaper under German administration - was smuggled into our cell. It reported that the German administration was allowing the Technical University of Warsaw to hold the final examinations for the Master's degree in engineering sciences. My classmates were going to graduate, while I sat in prison, probably facing execution. It was quite a bitter thought.

The public prosecutor taught us how to survive if we were transferred to a cell for criminal prisoners. It was interesting and instructive. It was customary for the criminal prisoners to test a newcomer by throwing a towel on the floor. The new prisoner, who usually was in prison for the first time in his life, usually would bend down and pick up the towel. That was the signal to the rest of the cell that the newcomer must be taught a lesson, a painful one. A seasoned prisoner would know to use the towel as a door mat, carefully clean his shoes with it, and then kick the towel aside. That was the sign that he belonged.

All in all, life in prison was not physically harsh. Of course, we dreamt about freedom and about fighting our enemies and the psychological pressure was immense. Four depressing things shaped life in the prison: the lack of mutual trust; rumours about the very brutal, often deadly, techniques of interrogation developed by the Gestapo officers; rumours that after interrogations we were likely to receive death sentences; and the fact that we would never know when our interrogation would happen. Afterwards, when in the concentration camp, I learned that all those factors had been carefully developed by the psychologists in service of the Gestapo, in order to break the spirit and will to fight of the prisoners and force them into submissiveness and despair. At that time, we only knew that we were dealing with a cruel and sadistic enemy. The calculatedness of it all began to become clear to me only when I was interrogated.

The lack of mutual trust was understandable. The methods of intelligence agencies are the same everywhere. At first, of course, the other prisoners did not trust me! There was a real possibility that I might be an informer. So they wanted to know who my father was, as well as my mother, my stepfather, where my mother taught, where my father worked, everything about my family. Fortunately, the judge knew of my father, so then I was accepted as legitimate and the tension eased after that. Still, it took about two weeks for me to gain the confidence of my fellow prisoners. Unfortunately, I spoiled the atmosphere of trust when I attempted to help a new prisoner who was put into our cell. He was a peasant from a small village in the Transcarpathian Ukraine and did not speak Polish. He was terrified because nobody could understand him and his behavior indicated that he clearly believed that he was surrounded by deadly enemies. He spoke a kind of Ukrainian dialect that I could just barely understand. I felt pity for him and, after a long while, I asked him in Ukrainian: "Where are you from?" The effect was tantamount to a thunderclap. The terrified Ukrainian chap relaxed, smiled and became talkative, but my fellow prisoners froze – I had used the language of our worst enemy. It took several weeks for me to regain the trust of the cell.

The rumours about the cruelty of interrogations were quickly confirmed for us. Several prisoners had died during the interrogations. We did figure out that one of the methods of interrogation was to break the eardrums, so all of us, with the kind assistance of the Polish guards, acquired a piece of cotton to put into our ears before the interrogation. In this way, we could protect our eardrums a bit. This was quite a small consolation, but it served to raise the spirit.

It was particularly stressful not knowing the date of the coming interrogation. We knew that one day each of us would be interrogated by the Gestapo officers and we knew that the interrogation would be certainly stressful, probably painful, perhaps even deadly. It is very difficult to maintain one's peace of the mind when one had to expect to be called by the Gestapo any time. True, the interrogation techniques of the NKVD or of the KGB were known to be cruel, perhaps even crueler, and it was common knowledge the Soviet security services customarily conducted interrogations at night when the prisoner's psychological resistance was at its lowest level. We discussed all this, but somehow it was not a consolation.

So, the period of time between my arrest in February 1940 and April 1940 when the interrogations started, was a difficult time. The only interesting events were the arrivals of new prisoners. I remember one such case, besides the arrival of that peasant from the Transcarpathian Ukraine. He was a peasant from a small Polish village. He was completely bewildered and could not understand why he was arrested by the Gestapo. He had never been involved in politics and in any military affairs. All that he had done was, in his words, to put a "nice piece of steel" in his barn. He hoped to use it to barter with the local blacksmith for new hinges for the barn door or maybe a new blade for his plough. When I asked him what kind of "piece of steel" it was, he replied, in the rural Polish dialect, "A very small tank, sir, a very small tank." The Polish army was using very small, one-person tanks for reconnaissance purposes at that time. That tank had broken down and been abandoned. For a peasant, living in a small remote village, the steel in that tank represented a veritable treasure. He was not interested in the military value of a tank, but he was very interested in the steel it contained, and he had intended to make use of that steel on his farm. After about two months, he disappeared. Perhaps the Gestapo finally understood the mentality of a small farmer living in village far away from a city, who had been born into a tradition of recycling everything, and had released him. Perhaps not.

Despite the tense atmosphere in the cell and the sense of being caught in another world, the traditional patterns of a very stratified Polish society were still visible. I remember a very young, tall man, less than twenty years old, who told us that his name was Kilometr, which was unlikely. He apparently came from the city of Poznan and certainly was forced to leave that part of Poland when it was incorporated into the Third Reich. When one of the older prisoners in the cell asked him what his father did in Poznan, he answered that his father was a janitor in an apartment building. The immediate reaction on the part of the professionals in the cell was one of disdain and dismissal. The young man defended himself and his father by saying that the profession of a janitor was as decent and honorable as any other profession, but the old prejudices were still strong.

So, I took a stand and supported that young man, reminding my fellow prisoners that in Pilsudski's Legions there was no difference between a street urchin and a count – both were citizens with the same rights. Even though I was one of them, a member of the Polish intelligensia, a commander of a detachment of the respected *Zwiazek Strzelecki* and an officer of the Polish army wounded in action, my words fell on deaf ears – the old feudal customs die hard. With some chagrin, I also had been guilty of the same prejudice – when I was younger and had invited one of my girlfriends to a students' ball, I tried to warn her obliquely not to mention that her parents owned a grocery store, something considered slightly déclassé in Polish society at the time.

The atmosphere in the cell altered when, in April 1940, the first prisoner from our cell, the major, was taken for interrogation. After several hours, he returned, unharmed. As I remember, he told us that he was not physically abused, but that the interrogation was tough. The crucial question, posed to him as a physician, was how he would prioritize the treatment of wounded Polish and German soldiers on the battlefield– which soldier would he treat first, the Polish soldier or the German soldier. I expected him to have answered that he would treat the most serious cases first, based on the principles of triage, but his answer had been something very different. He had told his interrogators that he would have treated the Polish soldiers first, before the German soldiers. I was shocked, especially after the way the German medical staff had treated me when I had been shot down. I understood that the major was fiercely patriotic, but I also thought that a physician should be above the politics of the war. It also seemed certain that the major had signed his own death sentence. After that, I do not remember when the other prisoners were taken for interrogation. All I remember was that the prisoners returning from the interrogation slept and were allowed to sleep, for a very, very long time, often up to twenty-four hours.

I think that it was the end of April when I was called to get ready for interrogation. By then, I expected the moment would come soon, but I was still taken by surprise. As a result, I forgot to put pieces of cotton into my ears to protect my hearing against damage during the interrogation. The guard did not speak to me, just gestured to me with his gun. And all I could do was worry about my hearing.

We had to walk outside of the prison, to the Gestapo headquarters, which were in another part of the city. It was not far, about one-and-a-half kilometres, or twenty minutes. However, to me it was an eternity. It was also surreal, because after months in my prison cell, I was walking through another world, the world outside the prison walls, where ordinary, free people lived, walked, laughed. The streets seemed full of young, pretty girls, dressed attractively, the sun was shining – it was bizarre. It was a paradise, but not for me. I did not know whether I would be able to walk back to the prison on my own legs or even whether I would return to my cell alive.

When we got to the headquarters, I was taken to a large room with a large, wooden table in the middle. A young woman, perhaps in her twenties, lay on her stomach on top of the table. I was ordered to stand against the wall near the table, facing the wall and close enough that my nose touched it, to put my hands straight down at my sides, to keep my eyes open and not to move. After few minutes the wall started spinning, but I did not dare close my eyes. It was difficult to maintain my balance. My guard left the room. I was left alone, except for the young woman who was silent behind me.

A few minutes later two men entered the room. They spoke in German, a language I did not yet understand. After a while, I heard a crack of a whip and the sound of it cutting into flesh. The girl cried out. I was stunned. A woman was being tortured just behind my back and I was doing nothing. I had been taught since a small boy that one of my first duties was to protect women and children without hesitation, but now a woman was in deadly distress, needed protection, and I, twenty-five years old and strong, was doing nothing. It was a horrible dilemma. The sounds of the lashes became rhythmic, and the loud shrieks of the girl changed into quieter groans. I felt some wet spots falling on my neck. Her blood splattered the wall around me, it hit me on the back of my head, on my back. It seemed an eternity while they tortured her just behind me. To me, it was an incredible torture to be forced to listen and know there was nothing I could do to prevent it. It may sound cowardly, but I was really happy when the door at my left opened and a young man in civilian clothes, not much older than myself, appeared and said to me, in Polish, that I should follow him to a second room. I presume he was Volksdeutsch – a Polish citizen of German origin who had declared allegiance to the Third Reich and who was serving as an interpreter.

The second room was much smaller than the first room. Again there was a table in the middle of the room, but no one was on top of this one. Two Gestapo officers were sitting at the table. On the wall in front of me was a bizarre display. Hanging on about thirty iron hooks was a vast array of different types of weapons, ranging from heavy, bone-breaking clubs, to lighter sticks, about two centimetres thick; from chains encased in leather, to very thin elastic wires and springs that could cut skin and muscle like butter. It was quite a collection. Both SS officers sized me up and, after a long while, one of them gave me an order, immediately translated into Polish by the interpreter – I was to select the whip that suited me most.

I do not remember what happened afterwards, not even to this day. I have tried to recall it, but to no avail. The next thing I can remember is that it was much later in the day, because the light was already gray. I was back standing up against the wall in the first room, in the same place and in the same position I had been when they had tortured the young woman, with my nose up against the wall. I remember, other than myself, the room was empty; the girl had disappeared from the table. After a while, my interpreter reappeared, told me to turn around and asked me one question, whether or not I was a military pilot. I replied that I was simply a glider pilot, which was the truth. He said something that sounded like, "This is good," and left the room. After a short while, a guard appeared to return me to the prison. I have no idea how I managed to get back, I do not remember the walk at all. I do not even remember returning to my cell or how my fellow prisoners greeted me. I only remember that I awoke in the evening of the next day and was told that I slept more than twenty-four hours.

By the end of April or early May, all of us had been interrogated. With that particular torment over, the atmosphere in the cell altered significantly. There was nothing we could do or say to alter the decision being made about our fates in Berlin. So, in a strange sense of the word, we relaxed and looked for ways to divert our attention. Unfortunately, none of us knew poetry well, so our attempts to enjoy the beauty of words and find some superior meaning in life were unsuccessful. Perhaps the possible death sentences hanging over our heads impaired our ability to enjoy poetry. Nonetheless, we hit upon another means of diversion. True, it was simple, even primitive, but it worked and helped us to maintain our morale. I do not remember who thought of it, but while the prosecutor and the major approved, the priest was horrified. Our diversion was simple, we "organized" a ouija board. I was interested in playing with it, because I confidently expected to be able to expose the fraud it was, given my scientific education. It was a simple thing to organize. We already had a table in the cell. We simply needed a china plate, a large piece of paper and a pencil. We put the large sheet of paper on the table, and drew on it two circles, one inside the other, both larger than the plate. In the space between the inner and outer circles, we wrote the letters of the alphabet and the numbers from one to nine, so it looked something like the face of a clock, with the dish, upside down, in its centre, with a large arrow drawn on its rim.

We took our places around the table and created a circle around the table with our hands, touching little fingers and thumbs together. One of us kept one hand free, to act as scribe. The priest refused to participate, stating that this was a work of Satan and decided to read his breviary sitting in a corner of the cell, while we 'worked' the board. All our fingers were supposed to be suspended just above the plate, without touching it. We were asked to concentrate. I concentrated on observing the fingers – watching to see whether or not someone touched the dish. After a long while, the prisoner who held the pencil asked questions. As I watched closely, the dish started to move in a circular motion. No one was touching the dish! It was obvious that the dish could not move without a supply of energy, but nobody touched the dish and it still moved. Moreover, the dish spelled out words that formed sentences that answered the questions! It was incredible, but I could not find any evidence of any cheating, not once during the several times we tried this.

The other diversion that we came up with was some experimentation with hypnosis. The major, as a physician, was well acquainted with hypnosis and decided to share with us his knowledge. His explanations made it clear that we were very susceptible to strong suggestions because of our psychological state – each of us had had to come to terms with the reality of our situation – that there were only two possible outcomes, we were either going to be executed soon or sentenced to a slow death in a concentration camp. With the exception of the priest, who evidently hoped that the Vatican would take steps to set him free, nobody expected to be released, so, while waiting for death, we tried to divert our attention from our destiny. As we had had no personal experience with hypnosis, we were interested in learning about it.

The first step was simple. The major told us to sit down, to interlace the fingers of both our hands and completely relax. After a while the major inspected our hands pressing the fingers even closer. A few minutes later, he told us that we would not be able to unclench our fingers, but should try to do it. I did not believe him, but he was right – my hands stayed clenched. So I concentrated on my hands and slowly, very slowly, I was able to release them and then I looked around. The faces of my fellow prisoners had shown surprise. All hands remained clenched, but one younger prisoner panicked and started hitting his knees with his clenched hands. The Major quickly approached him, took his clenched hands into his own hands, told him that he may separate his hands and he did it, with a very strange expression on his face. Then the Major selected one of the more suseptible prisoners and put him into a deep hypnotic sleep. I was skeptical, but when I saw the sleeping prisoner eating an onion eagerly because the Major told him that he was eating an apple, I changed my mind. The Major explained that the sleeping person would obey any order, provided that the order did not violate his moral code. In such a case, the hypnotized person would have a dangerous hysterical attack. I still don't understand the phenomenon, although I have tried to. However, I also cannot accept the priest's belief that Satan was behind these things.

Life in the prison was quiet at that time, with one exception. Knowing that they had nothing to lose, the prisoners in a few cells decided to organize an uprising and escape. They broke the cell doors, broke the doors to the exercise yard, but got no further. They were not able to break through the main prison gate and after a few hours, all of them were back in their cells. I don't recall that the Gestapo punished the mutinous prisoners. Perhaps the impending sentences were considered sufficient.

At the end of June, the Gestapo received the sentences approved by the Reichsminister Heinrich Himmler and ordered the prisoners to get ready for their departure. Each of us, as required by German law, was given our sentence to read and sign, although I had only a minute to look at mine. I was described as a Polish legionary, and my sentence was an ominously vague, "Return Undesired." As I recall, there were three groups of prisoners – the prisoners to be released (a very small group); the prisoners to be executed (by far, the largest group); and the prisoners sentenced to a concentration camp, who were to be sent to a collecting prison in the city of Tarnow. I found myself in the third group. To the best of my knowledge, nobody else from my cell was in that group. Rumor had it that the prisoners sentenced to death were executed that same day in the prison yard.

The rest of us were taken to the train station – one of us was put in chains, Lolek Krasnodebski. I don't recall why he was in irons, but he was a scion of an old Polish family and a student in the Law Faculty of Warsaw University. Lolek would become a good friend of mine in the concentration camp. He was extremely talented, very brave and had an insatiable intellectual curiosity. At the train station, we were put on a regular passenger train, in third-class carriages. I looked around for an escape route, but there was none. The only place where I could be alone was the toilet, but the toilet window was locked. The route to Tarnow was through a beautiful part of Poland, the Carpathian Mountains. The scenery was lovely - woods, broken by small farmfields, old villages, very old medieval towns, and laced with clean creeks. There is a sense of freedom in the hills that can't be found in the plains. It was difficult to accept the fact that I no longer belonged there.

The prison in Tarnow was very different from the one we had just left. It was a relatively modern one. We were put into a cell, number 59, with two or three bunkbeds in it. There was no toilet in this cell, instead we called a guard when we needed to go to the toilet, as well as had three scheduled visits daily. There were two small windows in this cell, high up the wall opposite the door. Unlike before, these windows were not boarded up, but covered with heavy steel bars. In this cell, I could see the sky! And if you jumped and grasped the bars, you could haul yourself up and not only see the sky, but you could also see the street and the women walking there, the free people walking in the street, living their lives. So close and yet so far. You could not stay long like this, it was too hard, and besides somebody had to watch the door because it was strictly illegal to do this. It was also very depressing, for it seemed that I was on a different planet from those people passing by on the street. So I went 'sightseeing' very seldom.

The Polish prison administration was courteous, but it was visibly under the strict supervision of the Gestapo. Books were available from the prison library if you wished to read. If we did get a book from the library, however, we had to ensure that we did it openly. We had to be careful not to make the impression that we were attempting to smuggle an illegal note. The food, however, was disastrously inadequate and we were hungry all the time, unlike the previous jail. After a few weeks, the Polish Red Cross began to send to each of us, once a week, a two-kilogramme loaf of dark rye bread – it was delicious and made an enormous difference, because the food remained poor for the whole time of our stay there.

In spite of the poor food, the mood of the prisoners gradually improved. Most importantly, since we had already been sentenced, there were no more interrogations, so we were mercifully spared the screams of those being tortured that had punctuated the night in the first jail. We knew that our life expectancy in a concentration camp would be about three months, but I was young, strong and I hoped that I would stay alive until the time arrived when I would be able to strike back. At that time, I lost all respect for the Germans. They were not the same Germans that I knew from literature, poetry, scientific and engineering books and from personal contacts. Certainly, they were no longer the proverbial nation of poets and philosophers. They were a goal-oriented, pragmatic people who put expediency over principles by surrendering their own value system to the will of their *Führer*. Their new goal, to assure a glorious future of the German nation by using all possible means, including the extermination of actual and potential opponents of their concept of national happiness, was repulsive. True, I remember individual officers and soldiers who deserved my respect, but I began to realize that they were rare exceptions, not the rule. The

Gestapo were the norm, as were their rules. This is what I learned in the prison in Tarnow.

We fell into the same kind of pattern as we had developed in the first jail, to pass the time and keep our spirits up. We sang Polish military songs, starting with the 14th century song, "Mother of the God", a song that was sung by the Polish and United armies before the battle at Grunwald in 1410. Lolek, who was not a devout man, nonetheless taught us a recent religious song, "We want God." At one point, I mentioned that I had learned the technique of hypnotism, and my fellow prisoners wanted to try it. Ignoring the possible dangers, figuring nothing could be more dangerous than the concentration camps to which we were doomed, I agreed to try it. I used the same routine as that used by the major in Sanok. I selected the most susceptible prisoners and began a series of sessions. I asked several questions, mostly related to our future. Of course, none of us believed that the answers, but it was good entertainment. However, one of the sessions took a decided turn for the worse, and it is still vivid in my memory. One evening, Lolek asked to try the hypnosis, saying that he wish to ask some questions. After putting one of our colleagues into a hypnotic sleep, I allowed Lolek to ask questions. To my surprise and consternation, Lolek went too far. He asked whether he would die in concentration camp. The answer was yes. The next question was how he would die. The answer was "on an elevation", which Lolek interpreted as on a hill. Then he asked whether there were dead leaves on the ground or not, in an attempt to determine in what season he would die. The answer was "I see many fall leaves". Then Lolek asked one final question, "Look at the leaves and read the numbers that are there." The answer was forty-three. I decided to stop this session at this point, because it had taken a nasty turn and had made all of us strongly subdued – the questions and answers were too specific, too disturbing and too forboding. Fortunately we forgot it quickly.

I had cause to remember this session three years later, in the fall of 1943. At that time I was working in the Baubüro or Construction Office in the concentration camp, as well as part of the camp's Resistance organisation. Lolek was working as a nurse in the camp hospital. One evening, Lolek told me that he had evidence showing how some homosexuals were forcing teenagers to serve as their sexual toys using drugs and that he was going to expose them the next day. The youngest prisoners were twelve years old, so for those homosexuals who were unable or unwilling to control their urges and willing to use drugs to make the children compliant, the concentration camp was a sort of sexual paradise. It was clear to me how dangerous the situation was and I offered Lolek protection. Lolek refused, stating that he wished to deal with this alone and I, stupidly, accepted his request not to provide him with extra security. I have no excuse for my stupidity, only an explanation. I knew very well how ambitious Lolek was and I did not want to hurt his feelings. The next day, early in the morning, well before the morning reveille, one of our Resistance group, working in the camp hospital, came to my barracks and woke me up. I looked at him and asked "Lolek?" He answered "Lolek." So, Lolek Krasnodebski, my dear friend, a good freedom fighter, a brave man and an outstanding intellectual, was murdered, injected with drugs and hanged, during a night in the fall of 1943.

It was either 8 or 9 August 1940, when the prison guards ordered us to take all our belongings and go to the prison square. We were allowed to take our bread and a metallic cup. There was a pump in the square, thus we were not thirsty. After a long while, the prison guards put us on the open trucks with benches, and gave the order to sit on the benches quietly, without movement and without speaking. Shortly afterwards the trucks pulled out – we were on our way to the concentration camp. The route to the railroad station was through the city. The day was warm and sunny and the streets were full of people – mostly women, girls and children. They seemed from another world; this was no longer our city, nor our planet. We did not belong. We were in an entirely different category – driving through the city without belonging to it and looking down on the city people from the height of the trucks. It reminded me of the Cossacks, and others, who had been taken to their death in tumbrells, carts, riding high above the crowd, as a warning.

The train consisted of ten cattle cars and two personal carriages, at the front and at the end. The prisoners were put into the cattle cars, fifty prisoners per car. I entered my car together with my friends from prison and the door was locked behind us. The car was empty and acceptably clean when we entered it. There were two small, barred windows in one wall, which allowed some light and some air to enter the car. However, the day was warm, the windows were small, so it was soon sweltering inside. Fortunately, only young people were in our car and we arranged it so that everybody could spend few minutes at the window, so nobody died during the journey. The car was far too small to allow fifty persons to lie down and so we rotated, some standing so that others could sit for a spell.

Before long the train started to move and we were on the last leg of our journey to the German concentration camp, KZ Sachsenhausen. At that time we identified the concentration camps with the German nation. It took us a while to realize that we were wrong – the concentration camp should be identified with the system, not with the nation. After all, the first prisoners in the concentration camps had been Germans, as early as 1933, and they had been subjected to quite cruel treatment, often resulting in death.

I do not remember how long the journey was. The distance from Tarnow to Berlin is not far, a train starting at noon one day could arrive the next morning, but I remember that our train stopped many times at small stations, so it is likely that our journey lasted close to two days. However, I do remember that I was thinking about escape. One of the boards in the floor of our car was loose, which meant that we could lift the boards in the floor of the railcar. Whenever the train approached a rail station, it slowed down as it passed through, so it seemed possible to drop out of the railcar at one of those points. After all, I knew that there was no return from the KZ, so it was simply a matter of risking death now versus the certainty of death later. I approached my friends and told them of my plan, and they seemed convinced. I asked them if they would join me. The first answer was yes; the second answer was yes; the third answer was yes. Then, someone hesitated, and said, "I vote for escape." The hesitation was enough. The enthusiasm was shattered. Everyone had to agree to the attempt wholeheartedly, or we could not do it, morally, because a successful escape was a death sentence for anyone left behind. We could only do it if those remaining behind agreed to the attempt, fully aware of the consequences they would be facing themselves. And the opportunity slipped by.

Eventually, the train arrived at a small railroad station, the car door was unlocked and we were ordered to get out - fast. It was my first exposure to the word *Schnell* – "fast". This word haunted, shaped my life, for the next five years. I jumped out of the car and looked around. The railroad station was small and neat. There was a sign on the station building – Sachsenhausen. The train was surrounded by SS, with small metallic skulls on their caps – the emblem of the infamous SS-Totenkopfverbände, an organisation especially trained to guard the concentration camps. (*This was the notorious SS Deaths Head Division.*) The guards barked their orders at us in loud and angry voices, as if we were deaf and mutinous. We were ordered to form a column five rows deep and then we were counted. Nobody had escaped, nobody had stayed in a car, nobody had died, so the number was indeed five hundred. Then there were two short, abrupt commands bellowed at us: "Turn right! March!" and we were in motion, with "Schnell, schnell!" ringing in our ears. We marched through a pine forest. You could soon see a high white wall ahead, with barbed wire on top. As we marched down the road, I was studying the terrain, because I was trying to decide whether to run for the forest. But no, not knowing the surroundings, I decided not to try. In that short distance, we passed several groups of men doing some work and guarded by the SS soldiers. All of them made a strange impression. They were slim, tanned and dressed in a sort of pyjamas and a strange round cap. The pyjamas and caps were made of an apparently stiff fabric, white or grayish white with wide, blue, vertical stripes. Interestingly, our presence did not attract their attention – we might as well have been invisible. We walked along the wall for a while and then turned to the right – before us was a gatehouse with an elegant, hand-forged iron gate. A large sign, clearly visible, was on the gate: "Arbeit macht frei" – "Labor Brings Freedom". We passed through the gate, being counted again very carefully, and entered the Konzentrationslager Sachsenhausen.

Sachsenhausen (1944)

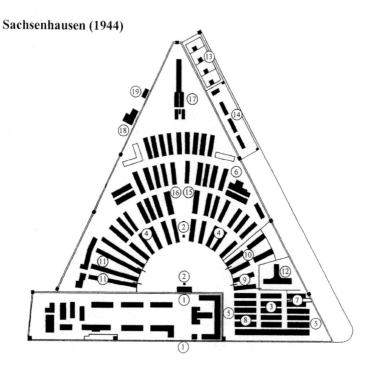

Legend:
1. Entrance
2. Gallows
3. Barracks
   38 & 39 (Jewish prisoners)
4. Barracks
   38 & 39 (Jewish prisoners)
5. Quarantane or Isolation
6. Delousing Station
7. Barrack 58 (Isolation for special political prisoners)
8. Forgery Workshops
9. Penal Barrack
10. Camp for Soviet prisoners of war
11. Camp hospital
12. Cells
13. Special Operations
14. Camp for officers & soldiers of Western Allies
15. Prisoner Kitchen
16. Laundry
17. SS Garden & Pigsty
18. Crematorium: Station Z
19. Execution Ground

Part Two

The First Two Years

The concentration camp system into which Pindera found himself thrown in the spring of 1940 was already well-developed by that time. There had been concentration camps in Germany since 1933, when the SS, SA and Gestapo all established detention camps to hold the thousands of German Communists, Social Democrats, trade unionists and other 'political enemies' of the State who were caught in the waves of arrests that marked the Nazis' ascent to power. By 1936, the SS had seized control of the concentration camps and had revamped them not just administratively, but also physically - shutting down the smaller, temporary and less efficient camps, and constructing new, purpose-built and larger permanent camps. Control over the camps gave the SS significant control of the policing of the country, an important power in its own right. However, by this time, Himmler and the SS also had come to realize that these camps, as an important source of labour, could play an important part in consolidating the organisation's position of power in the new Germany, both during wartime and in peace. If the SS controlled access to this labour force, which was key to the success of the monumental construction projects of the pre-war years and armaments needs of the Reich during the war, it both could profit financially from the lease of prisoners and the sale of the product of their work, as well as be in a position of considerable influence and power. This is why Sachsenhausen was located where it was - close to a major population centre, certainly, but also because of rich clay deposits nearby which could be used for brickmaking. Indeed, the Sachsenhausen brickworks were a major source of revenue for the SS throughout the 1930s. The purpose of this camp, then, was not the immediate elimination of its prisoner population, unlike the special extermination camps built later. Its initial stated purpose was the 're-education' of its inmates, but its primary purpose, by the end of 1937, as made clear in an order issued by Himmler on 14 December 1937, was the ruthless exploitation of their labour. This is not to dismiss the hell that was the camp system. These prisoners' labour was extracted brutally, with no consideration to the ultimate health of the working population, and with death often the result. A prisoner could be killed instantly, on the whim of a guard, or literally worked to death. The mortality rate in Sachsenhausen was appalling. Productivity was raised by working the prisoners harder, not by using their labour more efficiently. Terror and punishment ensured productivity, the SS reasoned. Many of the SS seemed to take perverse pleasure in literally working the prisoners to death. This, combined with the extremely poor food, and little of it, the deplorable working and living conditions, and the almost non-existent medical care, meant the mortality rate was appallingly high. Some estimates place it at 50 or 60%.

By 1937, there were more than 2500 such prisoners in Sachsenhausen, many of whom had been leading civil servants, politicians or intellectuals in Germany. Polish nationals began arriving soon after that country's invasion on 1 September 1939. By the time Pindera had arrived, the Polish prisoners in the camp outnumbered the German. The total population by August 1940 was very diverse. It numbered 12,867, and was made up of 4169 Polish political prisoners; 3564 German political prisoners, including Czechs from the Sudetenland; 2069 German asocial prisoners (designated as ASOs in the camp and included the homosexuals and socially deviant); 1268 German criminal prisoners (designated as BVs by the camp administration); 1212 Jewish prisoners and 450 Jehovah's Witnesses (the Bibelforscher).

After 1940, the number grew rapidly, especially of Polish prisoners. By the end of 1942, Sachsenhausen had more than 16,500 prisoners in the main camp from a wide range of nationalities - Slovaks, Poles, Hungarians, Rumanians, Greeks, Yugoslavians (mostly Serbians and Croatians), Norwegians, Latvians, Lithuanians, Estonians, Ukrainians, Russians, Arabs, Gypsies, Jews, stateless persons, to name a few. They were political prisoners, criminal prisoners, asocial prisoners, homosexuals, Jehovah's Witnesses, Jews and Gypsies. Pindera even remembers once meeting an American in the camp. Estimates are that approximately 200,000 passed through the gates of the main camp during its operations. By 1944, the camp population was almost 50,000. As well as the main camp, Sachsenhausen had approximately 100 satellite camps, located away from the main camp, which ranged from a barrack attached to a factory to a major industrial complex, like those at the airplane factories, Heinkelwerke and Messerschmittwerke. It is thought that some 500,000 prisoners were spread out in this network of camps.

Of course, it would be a while before Pindera would understand the camp and its inner workings. Initially, little made sense. This was the usual experience of the inmates. The camp 'system' was one intended to brutalize, terrorize. It was not intended to make sense to the prisoners and in that way, it would destroy their will, spirit, and to brutalize them. The lessons Pindera learned, gradually, were harsh ones.

Once we were in the camp's compound, the SS ordered us to stop. I looked around. On the surface, nothing looked odd, but still there was a strangeness to the place. The camp square in which we stood (I learned later that it was called the Appellplatz or Roll-Call Square) was clean. There was a wide path of concrete leading from the gate to the first building, otherwise it was covered with black cinder. Ringing the Appellplatz were wooden barracks with gable walls facing the square. There was no litter anywhere, not even a piece of paper. The barracks were painted green and seemed very clean. These barracks were known as Blocks. There was a flower box on each gable of the first ring of barracks, filled with colourful flowers. And in the middle of the space was a beautiful flower garden, about 50 metres long! Above the flowers, across the eighteen gables, were painted in large letters the following words: "There is one path to freedom; its milestones are called obedience, industry, honesty, order, cleanliness, sobriety, truthfulness, sacrifice, and love of the Fatherland." I realized later that there was a bitter irony in the fact that the word "Love" was painted on the gable of the barrack numbered 18, where the Penal Kommando was housed, because a prisoner typically did not survive more than two weeks in that Kommando.

There were many prisoners around the grounds, doing various jobs. All of them wore peculiar striped clothing, and all of those who were not carrying a load of some sort were jogging. I soon learned that this was the norm, as the rule was "When in Camp, always on the double." All the prisoners were very slim and had a nice suntan. When passing an SS officer, they dropped to a walk and, well before passing the officer, removed their cap, holding it rigidly at their right side and only returning it to their heads several steps past the officer. I noticed that their hair was cut very short. When addressed by an SS officer, a prisoner assumed a position at attention, took off his cap and looked the officer straight in the eye. Much later I learned that it was very dangerous not to look into the eyes of an SS officer as the SS considered it as the sign of cowardice, something they deeply despised.

We stood at attention in the Appellplatz for a long while, and then were ordered to march off to the right, into the so-called Quarantäne Lager or Klein Lager – the Quarantine or Small Camp. It was also known as "Isolation". The quarantine camp consisted of eighteen numbered barracks, and was isolated from the main camp by a barbed wire fence and a barbed wire gate. The first step was registration. I had to state my name and date of birth and then I was handed a small piece of paper with a number on it. I was given 28 862 and was told to learn it by heart. Then we were sent to the Effects Room, where we left all our belongings which were put into sacks with our numbers. The one exception were our shoes, which we were allowed to keep. After that we were shaved. All the hair on my body was removed. Next, we were issued clothing - a shirt, undershorts, and the white-blue striped uniform consisting of pants, jacket and round cap. We were also allowed to have a spoon, toothpaste, toothbrush, a metallic bowl for eating, a cup, a small towel and piece of soap. Carrying our belongings, we were led then to a shower room. The day was warm, so being naked was not uncomfortable. Then we dressed and were brought back to the Quarantäne, quickly learning how to form the required columns five rows wide. Our group, five hundred men strong, was divided into two parts. One part was placed in Block 40. The second half, of which I was a part, was put in Block 59. There, I was asked to hand over the piece of paper with my number and I received two strips of fabric in exchange, about five centimetres by ten centimetres, with my number: 28 862. I was also given a cloth badge with a "P" on it, for Polish. These strips were different colours for different types of prisoners. As I was a political prisoner, I was given red badges, with a "P" on them. I was to sew the strips with the number and the red badges on my uniform – one on my breast and one on my thigh. This number became my name for the next five years.

We quickly found out that the life of prisoners in the concentration camps was closely governed by strict, often arbitrary regulations established by the SS administration. However, while the SS officers supervised all activities, the camp administration was made up of prisoners themselves, who were selected by the SS. The SS administration consisted of the Commandant in charge of the camp; a Lagerführer, his deputy, who himself had several deputies; a Rapportführer with his own deputies; numerous Blockführers, one for each prisoner block; numerous Bauführers responsible for the various

Kommandos or work crews; the camp physician; as well as other administrative personnel. All of these men were SS officers. All data on prisoners was kept in the Political Section or Office. The camp doctor was responsible for the health of the prisoners, and it was he who decided whether or not a prisoner was fit to receive a certain number of lashes as punishment. The main responsibility of the camp doctor was the camp's hospital. In Sachsenhausen, the hospital, which was called Revier, consisted of one major barrack, well equipped for emergency surgeries, and several hospital barracks. Only the prisoners in the Bunker, a very special prison within the camp, were outside the jurisdiction of the camp doctor. The Bunker was used for special disciplinary cases and few prisoners survived internment there.

In spite of this highly bureaucratic camp administrative structure, the SS believed that the prisoners should administer themselves. It relieved them of the tedium of the camp's daily management and provided a convenient scapegoat if anything went wrong. Paralleling the SS camp administration, then, there was a prisoner administration. The Kommandantur appointed three Lagerältester from among the prisoners, to run the prisoners' affairs and, especially, to manage the use of the prisoner labour force and allocate prisoners to work teams, or Kommandos. Below them, and appointed by them, were the Blockältesters, two for each barrack. These men ran the barrack, and closely supervised every aspect of the lives of the prisoners in their barrack. Below the Blockältester, to assist him in his supervisory task, came the Raumältester and the Tischältester, who ruled the dormitory and the table, respectively. The Lagerältesters appointed the foremen or Vorarbeiter for Kommandos, the prisoner medical staff for the hospital and the staff for the prisoner services, such as the kitchen and laundry. The Lagerältester were very powerful men, as were their subordinates, even if they were closely supervised by the SS.

Each barrack accommodated about three hundred prisoners in two wings, and was run by a Blockältester, who was a prisoner himself, assisted by two prisoners. A Blockältester in the Quarantäne had absolute power over the life or death of his prisoners. We also learned that, in the Quarantäne, each block was directly supervised by a Blockführer, who was an SS officer and a member of the SS Deaths Head Division, trained especially for that task.

We were introduced to our Blockführer during the first evening roll call. He was SS–Oberscharführer Wilhelm Schubert. His instructions were vital, but sobering. He announced that in the camp there are no sick persons. In camp there are only dead persons or living persons. He also made it clear that there was only one way out of the camp, and that was through the chimney of the crematorium. I will never forget his name as long as I am alive. He was a man who enjoyed his work. He was one of those SS officers who used to say, when talking about prisoners, that they were not humans, they were prisoners.

It was actually our Blockältester who checked the roll at evening roll call. He was a criminal prisoner, with a green triangle and a low number – about ten thousand. He was in his fifties, not tall but robust, with many pockmarks and evidently hardened by a long and brutal stay in the concentration camp. That first evening, he made it clear that he was not going to treat us softly. In fact, as we soon found out, he was able to be very brutal when he thought that the circumstances required it. However, he could also occasionally be almost humane. The roll call was done in the military style – upon command, the prisoners in the first row started counting, from zero to about sixty. The Blockältester walked along the columns to check the count and, after assuring himself that the number was correct, took his cap off his head, approached the Blockführer and reported that all prisoners were present. Having received the report, Schubert walked along our column, counting again. This would be the routine for the next five years.

After the evening roll call, we received our evening meal. Surprisingly, it was more satisfying than the meal in the Tarnów prison – which is more a comment on the meals at Tarnów than the meals at the KZ. During the meal and afterwards, before going to sleep, I met several of the older prisoners in my block. All of them were Polish and from the western part of Poland. They had been arrested in 1939. Nobody was very hopeful regarding our chances of surviving the KZ. I spent the rest of the evening exploring the block. It was a very simple building. There was a central room, where the washroom and washing fountains were located. It had four or six toilets and in the middle was a ring fountain, for washing ourselves. And there was a shower, but I believe only one. That was used for either punishment or for killing. We actually showered elsewhere. There was a hose, too, a normal garden hose, that produced a strong stream of water. That was used for cleaning, and often also for killing. It is a very easy way to kill someone and it is a very clean kill, because there is no blood, no trace of the death. It is easiest in the winter. You simply aimed a stream of cold water at a person's heart for ten or fifteen minutes. So that was the central part of the block. Off it were two wings - the sleeping and living quarters. Each wing was divided into two rooms, one for sleeping and one for our lockers, tables and the one source of heat, a stove. We used the stove for heat, certainly, but also to warm food and especially for drying wet clothes - a constant problem in the winter. This is where the Blockältester's bed was.

By ten o'clock, we were in the "dormitory", where we put straw mattresses on the floor, received one thin blanket per person and lay down. The room was so crowded that it was impossible to lie on our backs. So we had to lay on our sides, very close to each other. In one corner of the room were a number of cans, which we were to use as chamber pots during the night. The Blockältester had made it very clear to us that he did not wish to see anybody going to the toilet during the night. It disturbed his sleep because we would have to pass by him on the way to the toilets. Thus, everything had to be taken care of in the dormitory. Of course, the cans were never enough and, by the morning, the corner was always a foul mess. I believe it was that night that I met Janek Czapski. We ended up having to share a mattress, and figured out how we could sleep on the same mattress in such cramped quarters. You slept like spoons, nestled in a drawer. Janek and I ended up being very close friends, until he died several months later.

Life in Quarantäne was dominated by the Blockältester. The Blockältester for Quarantäne was chosen from among the most brutal of the criminal prisoners. His job, as was the job of his assistants, was to 'condition' the newcomers. It was a very important function, from the perspective of the SS, because he was the one who sorted out the incoming prisoners – between those who were likely to survive for a certain period of time and those who were likely to die quickly. His task was to accelerate the death of those he believed were not going to survive anyway, and to test those who might survive. This was done in a variety of ways. One such way was "Sport", or at least that was what they called it. It involved suddenly being ordered to run, in any and all directions; or being told to suddenly drop to the ground, roll in the dirt and jump to your feet again. Another favourite was being ordered to drop into a squatting position, and to hop like a frog, with your arms outstretched in front of you. This was very difficult and very tiring. So was another exercise – you were required to bend your knees and squat as low as possible, with your hands and arms straight out in front of you, and to stay like that for two hours. After fifteen minutes, your legs were numb, dead. And then after an excruciating two hours, you would be ordered to stand up, but many could not because the circulation to their legs had been cut off and it was very painful to straighten them. A common injury while in Quarantäne was swollen legs and feet. There were other ways of eliminating the weak too, such as the Stehkommando. We were required to stand in formation, without moving a limb or even our eyes, for hours – sometimes six, even twelve hours. And they would count and recount the prisoners, looking for someone to break formation, to move, to collapse. They would be killed instantly.

We were also subjected to physical inspections on an irregular basis. We were required by camp rules to bathe ourselves regularly, which we did mainly in the washing fountain in the barracks. We got weekly, sometimes bi-weekly showers, in the showerhouse. Although the water temperature fluctuated greatly, first tepid, then hot and then sometimes ice cold at the end, we enjoyed them. The parade of naked prisoners appealed to our rather dark sense of humour - later we called the trips to the showers, "The Dance of the Skeletons." The washing fountain, on the other hand, was only cold water, and so some people got lax in their personal hygiene. Most of us had realized the importance of bathing, even in the winter, because putting your hands, arms and back under water in the morning, regardless of the cold, was very helpful for blood circulation. Fewer were as diligent in washing from the waist down, although we were supposed to do that, as well. The Blockältester would spring surprise inspections on us, and he would use a long stick to "remind" those who had forgotten the importance of proper hygiene. Sometimes, when we were standing in formation, the Blockältester ordered us to hold our hands out in front of us for inspection. If he thought someone's hands were too soft, the mark of the elite, he pulled that person out of the line and they had to do two or three hours of sport. Many survived, some did not. When he came to me in the line, he was confused, because my face was not that of a worker, but my hands were hard from rowing at university, where I had been on the rowing team. He hesitated, and then looked at my face, and sent me to do Sport.

There were also other deaths and many of the original five hundred died in those first months. Some of the deaths were particularly cruel and painful, and used to instill terror and blind obedience in the prisoners. In one case, a prisoner had stolen a small piece of margarine and got caught. The Blockführer looked after this prisoner's execution, and he ensured that we all learned a lesson from it. We were all ordered into rows before our barracks, at attention, and were forced to watch the execution. The Blockführer stood the condemned man in front of us, and force-fed him a full pound of margarine. And then, to 'aid his digestion', because a man starving to death would become seriously ill from consuming so much margarine at once, he called for a blanket and four prisoners, who created a trampoline and had the prisoners toss the condemned man up into the air repeatedly. And then he was put on the ground and the Blockführer ordered the Blockältester to jump on his stomach, which he did, again and again. And then the Blockführer ordered the man lifted up by the hands. You could see that his upper belly was concave, but his lower belly was distended. Then the Blockführer ordered him suspended by his feet, and them by the hands, and back again. He did this until the man died. It was a very impressive lesson for the rest of us, and it encouraged us all to be very, very obedient.

Most of us had heard rumours about the camps before arriving, about the horrific conditions. What we were experiencing just confirmed our worse nightmares. There seemed to be no logic to it, just sheer, black, senseless terror. Back in Tarnow, we had guessed that we would be able to survive about three months in the KZ. However, when I got to Sachsenhausen, I found out that some of the inmates had already survived several years of internment! These were, of course, the German communists and trade unionists, who were the original prisoners in the camp. They had not survived because they were given special treatment, however, far from it. So this meant it was possible to survive! I had also noticed a qualitative difference between circumstances in the main camp, which I saw when we went to the shower room once a week, and those of the Quarantäne. Life was much harsher and brutal in Quarantäne than outside it, in the main camp. One difference was that the prisoners outside of Quarantäne worked, while we did not. Instead we had Sport. The brutality and the selections inside seemed random, cruel, and pointless. And I started wondering why. What I was seeing and experiencing made no sense, especially given what I knew about German culture. I eventually came to the conclusion that this sadistic system, and it was a system, was designed to break the spirit. Those who were acting as its sadists had been carefully chosen for the job, as not everyone could do what they did. So they were carefully selected, from among thousands, for this particular job. And their job was to break the spirit of the prisoners and instill a feeling of terror by creating an atmosphere of apparently random terror. However, it was not random, but carefully orchestrated. This meant, I concluded, that if the terror was designed, it could be resisted, and I began to look at the camp in a very different way than I had up to that point. I realized that there was a peculiar logic to the Blockältesters' actions. What they were engaged in was selected killing – and in the process, eliminating those who were not likely to be obedient servants of Nazism or who were not likely to survive the camp anyway. And, often as not, they were also not acting on their own volition, but because of orders from their superiors, the Blockführers. I remember once when Schubert told my Blockältester that he had ten prisoners too many. The next morning, ten were laying there, dead. So the terror was not spontaneous, it had a system to it. And that was the beginning of my own resistance.

It was some time in the fall of 1940, probably in late September, while still in Quarantäne, that those prisoners still remaining were finally put to work. Life soon fell into a routine that was military in its discipline. The reveille came at 4:15 a.m. in the summer and 5:15 a.m. in the winter. The prisoners had forty-five minutes to wash, dress, make their beds with military precision, visit the latrine and get breakfast, which was usually 1/2 litre of coffee and bread, perhaps with a bit of marmelade or watery soup. At 5 a.m., they were in formation outside the barrack, ready to march to the Appellplatz for morning roll call. There they were counted and, if all were accounted for, they were formed into work Kommandos and marched off to the worksite by their foremen. There they would work for ten, twelve, even fourteen hours, with a mid-day meal of watery soup and coarse bread brought to them, then marched back to the camp for evening roll-call. Those of their comrades who died that day were dragged back with the Kommando, to be accounted for at evening roll-call. Once dismissed from the Appellplatz, only then did they get supper. There was a free hour in which they could write letters, visit with friends, attend illegal church services, practice for a cabaret or just relax. Then they were ordered into the barracks, a curfew descended, and they were in bed. It was a long, hard day, made worse by the inadequate food and brutal treatment.

Over the next year and a half, Jerzy Pindera worked in a variety of Kommandos, including a special type, called the Speer Kommandos, teams of slave labour which did particularly heavy, harsh and dangerous work. They were named after Albert Speer, Minister of Munitions and Industry, and the Kommandos were ostensibly intended to provide forced labour to the Ministry for its various projects. Pindera's sentence, "Return not desired", meant that he could only work on these Kommandos and only on those that worked outside. He was not allowed to work at a job under a roof. The purpose of the sentence, of course, was to work him to death. In his memoirs, the Kommandos all blur together and it is unclear how long he spent at

*any one of them. We do know that he remained housed in Barrack No.
59 until mid-June 1941. After then, he was moved out of Quarantäne
and into Barrack No. 16, where he remained until April 1942. What
Pindera does remember of the Speer Kommandos was the senseless
brutality of these work assignments and the system of terror continuing.
This lasted until he was recruited for the Baubüro, or Construction
Office, sometime in February 1942.*

One of the Kommandos to which I was assigned was clearing a
large site in a forest, in preparation for the construction of a weapons
factory. Our task was to remove the trees. Another Kommando was
actually felling the trees and trimming off the branches. Our
Kommando had the task of moving the trunks of the trees off to the
side and collecting the branches. All the roughage and the trunks were
being salvaged for the benefit of the nation, we were told. These were
very large pine trees, some had to be at least fifty years old. So the
trunks were very large and heavy. To move these trunks, we used
branches as poles, and put them under the trunk of the tree we wanted
to move. There would be ten teams of two prisoners, each with a pole,
and we would work them under the trunk so that, with a prisoner on
each side, the twenty of us could then lift the trunk. It was a very
primitive way of moving the trunks, but we could move it at a walk,
barely. This was also very dangerous, because if anyone lost their
balance, the heavy trunk would roll and could crush people. And, of
course, there were overseers who were criminal prisoners recruited
from Dachau. They had been given long sticks to use in order to
'encourage' or punish us. Every ten or fifteen metres, as we went past,
carrying the trunks, one of these overseers would randomly strike at us.
My friend, Tolek, was also on this Kommando. One time, he got on the
wrong side of one of the overseers, for some reason. The overseer
reported him to the Bauführer, who was in charge of the site. I can still
see Tolek standing in front of the Bauführer, stiff at attention with his
cap in his right hand as regulations required. The Bauführer tapped
Tolek on the forehead lightly and repeatedly, between the eyes, with
either a thin wooden rod or a piece of thick flexible metal wire. This, of
course, breaks the skin and breaks down the muscles there. Three
times, we passed the two of them, carrying a tree trunk. Tolek survived,
but the death rate on the Kommando was very high. Every day, when
we returned to the camp, we dragged back with us the corpses of those
who had died that day.

After a few days on this Kommando, I approached my
Blockältester. I told him, in my very broken German, that I could not

return to that Kommando the next day. I probably bribed him with something, although I do not recall what it might have been, and he transferred me to another Kommando. The work in the next Kommando was not as hard physically, but psychologically it was difficult. Underneath the administrative wing of the hospital was a special cellar where the corpses of the prisoners who died in the hospital were put. Our job was to carry the naked corpses from the cellar, where they had been dumped, to the crematorium, about a twenty-minute walk from the hospital. We were given a stretcher, and two of us carried corpses all day. We tried to give the corpses some dignity, but it was difficult. We were ordered to jog with the stretchers as the load was light. Each corpse only weighed about 45 to 55 kilogrammes. Because I was new to the Kommando and did not know where we were going, I was given the back end of the stretcher to carry, which was more awkward. It was also more disturbing because, when we jogged, the corpse would jump around on the stretcher in front of me. It was also important for the two of us to synchronize our steps and to adjust their length in order not to shake the corpse too much. We felt it was imperative to preserve the dignity of the corpse as much as possible. All day, I had to watch this spectacle of jostling corpses. Looking at the corpse was not always easy; sometimes the faces were contorted, anything but peaceful. I wondered whether the bearers carrying my corpse to the crematorium would feel the same compassion that I felt, and whether they would try to allow me some dignity in death.

We delivered the corpses to the crematorium, put them in a pile there, and others would actually feed them into the furnaces. And we did this round trip constantly, for there were always corpses to be delivered. There was a story about how one of the corpses woke up as it was being carried to the crematorium and no one knew what to do. He was already officially dead and so no longer existed as far as the administration went. I have no idea what happened to him, but I remember the tale.

The first bearer knew his way, so I just followed him without asking. We were forbidden to talk, so I was left with my thoughts. When we delivered the corpses, we entered a complex of buildings which contained the crematorium furnaces. We turned our stretcher over and dropped the corpse on a pile of other corpses, close to the furnace. I immediately turned to run back to the hospital, but my companion told me to relax. He explained that, although the Head of the Crematorium was an SS officer, he was not a Blockführer, and was in fact a decent man who did not mind if we took some minutes to rest between journeys. I relaxed, but only slowly, not ready to believe that we might truly be allowed to rest during working hours in the presence of an SS officer. Unbelievably, it was true. I took the moment to look around me and what I saw was impressive.

The crematorium furnaces were built in a row, side-by-side. I forget how many there were, maybe three, four or five. The furnaces were built of dark red fire-resistant bricks. The almost black cast-iron furnace doors were about one metre above the ground, which was covered by a light-gray dust mixed with very small pieces of white bones. The dust was human ash. There was a pile of corpses in front of the furnaces and two prisoners were assigned to each furnace. Corpses were loaded into the furnace by means of a device which we called a pan or spoon. It was a kind of steel stretcher. The pan rested on a steel support in front of the furnace, perpendicular to it. The two men picked up a corpse from the pile and put the corpse on the pan, head first. They opened the furnace door and the corpse was quickly slipped into the furnace. Then the pan was pulled from the furnace, the door was closed, and a new corpse was loaded onto the pan. After about three minutes, another corpse was put in. I think that I would have been shocked by this scene if I had seen it immediately after my arrival at the KZ. However, in the meantime I had seen so much human suffering, so much killing and so many dying and dead men, that the whole procedure of the final dispatching of prisoners "through the chimney", as we said in camp parlance, appeared almost humane to me and its efficiency appealed to my engineering mind. Strangely, there was no trace of that nasty smell of burning human flesh, which was so unpleasant and constantly present in the main camp, just a few hundred metres away. Evidently, the engineers who designed the crematorium had done a professional job. However, those engineers could not influence the colour of the smoke, which carried information disclosing one of the many secrets of the camp. When the regular prisoners were burned, the smoke was light-grey because there was no fat in the corpses. However, the smoke was dense and black when well-nourished people were burned, people who were brought directly to the crematorium from outside the camp.

Looking farther I noticed several other buildings and structures, much of which was under construction and which were mysterious to me. During following trips, I learned that they served various purposes, but all were related to the efficient killing of prisoners and the collection of their property. The main building was not yet completed. As I learned two years later, when that building was completed, it contained, among other things, a gas chamber disguised as a shower room and another room for execution disguised as a medical examination room.

Another building, called Kanada, was a storehouse for the clothes of the men, women and children who were delivered directly to the crematorium, bypassing the registration in the camp. Those unregistered people simply disappeared through the chimney, but their clothes remained. The clothes also contained money in various currencies, gold, jewellery and so on, sewn into the hems and seams, so the clothes were valuable and were well protected. Where the word "Kanada" came from, I do not know. Whatever its origins, it came to have an important meaning in the camp, for Kanada meant richness in camp parlance. It was a special, carefully supervised Kommando who sorted the clothes and looked for the valuables. There was also a special underground installation consisting of a small bunker for a machine gun and a wide walk leading underground, and it was used for group executions and for special kinds of individual executions.

Over the course of the day, we made a number of trips back and forth. Each time, my companion and I took some rest close to one of the crematorium furnaces, which radiated much needed and most enjoyable warmth. There was still no rain, so my back was dry and my feet were dry and warm. It was almost a paradise. Nonetheless, when the day and roll call were over, I washed myself more carefully than usual and I managed to get another work assignment the next day. It was not my last contact with the crematorium, however. A few weeks later, I had to return there on a personal mission. My friend, Janek, had died in my arms the night before, just before reveille. Rather than let him suffer the indignity of being dragged by the heels from our block to the crematorium, my Blockältester permitted me to carry him there on my back.

Another Kommando to which I was assigned was pulling stumps at a building site. It was December and the ground was frozen. One day, we were trying to pull an enormous stump and it was being very difficult. We had already dug a hole about one metre deep and I was in it. The soil was sandy and the frozen earth around me broke and fell on me, pinning my legs. I yelled for help and the other prisoners pulled me from the earth, but my legs were both hurt badly and my knees quickly swelled. The pain was atrocious and I saw stars in the middle of the afternoon! At the end of that day, the others helped me return to the camp and to my block. You see, I had to be able to stand and walk or the guards would have shot me immediately. When back at the camp, I somehow managed to make it out to evening roll call, but the Blockführer saw me and my injuries, and began to kick at my feet. Amazingly, the Blockältester stopped him and told him that I had had an accident and that was why I could not stand at attention properly. And he took me on his back and carried me to the hospital. I do not know why he did that, except that, perhaps, he knew that I was fighting to stay alive and admired that. He also came to visit me in the hospital, to tell me that a friend of mine, Waclaw Plonski, had died. When he told me, it was with compassion and a sad smile. It was the strangest thing. This man who killed people regularly, who had been selected especially for that task, was still capable of compassion. The concentration camp was a very complex reality.

Fortunately nothing had been broken in my legs, otherwise I would have been shot. Still, I was released from the hospital too early and my knees were still badly swollen, and I could barely walk. That should have been the end of me, but the Blockältester let me stay in the block under the category of 'bedrest' until I was able to walk.

One of the earlier Kommandos was the SS Hauser. I know it was one of the earlier ones because I was still a bit careless. The task was a very simple one. We were digging trenches to lay the foundations for a building. The soil was sandy and we were moving it from the construction site to another place, using a narrow gauge railway with a cart. The carts derailed easily and when they did, the prisoners pushing the cart had to lift it back on the tracks using a heavy stick. Without this crude lever, you would never have got it back on the rails. Each cart was pushed by four prisoners and the dumping ground was about half a kilometre away. When we had a load, we could walk. When the cart was empty coming back, we had to run – not jog, but run.

I became careless on this particular Kommando. In order to keep our spirits up, we were singing national anthems. Somebody began with the Polish national anthem, then someone sang the French one. When my turn came, I sang "God Save the King". This should not have been a risky thing to do because we were being careful to not sing them where the Germans would hear us, but one of the SS officers heard my song and reported me to the Bauführer. Well, to sing the national anthem of the enemy during wartime....! So the Bauführer confronted me and demanded to know what I had been singing. I told him that I had been singing a religious tune. He asked me which one, and I told him that I had forgotten already. So the Bauführer decided to refresh my memory with a length of finger-tip-wide telephone cable. It was extraordinarily painful, that whipping, and I was furious with myself because I knew there was an Austrian song that had the same tune as

"God Save the King", but I could not remember it. My mother had taught it to me when I was a small boy. I remember that the SS officer who had denounced me watched beating and he was shocked by what was happening, but he did nothing. Then the Bauführer let me go, as it was lunchtime, and my friends told me the name of the song. So when he came back, I "remembered." He was not happy. Later, on the same Kommando, we were moving boards and once, some boards fell on my arms and they bent under the weight. Our bones were that soft from the lack of vitamins and minerals. The Bauführer saw it and smiled. He was satisfied, because I had finally been punished properly.

At one point, Pindera was assigned to the Strafkompanie, or SK, which was an especially dangerous assignment. Prisoners assigned to it rarely survived more than two weeks. It was housed in a special block of the Quarantäne and the Blockältester was August Sievertsen. He was a quiet man, but his blows were deadly. However, he was not the worst of the experience. It was the Blockführer, SS-Hauptscharführer Richard Bugdalle, who decided when and how a particular member of the SK would die. His nickname among the prisoners was Brutalla. He was a tall man and very strong, and he took pride in his ability to kill a man with his hands and his feet. He did so frequently, calmly and methodically, without expression. Pindera recalled that the members of the SK were easily recognized, not just because they were always running, even when carrying a heavy load, but because they were marked with a black round circle, about five centimetres in diameter, in the middle of their backs, and by the haunted expression on their faces. Pindera was assigned to this Kommando by happenstance, as was the way of life in the camp. Luck, and being in the right place at the right time, or in the wrong place at the wrong time, could easily mean the difference between life and death.

As I remember it was a warm spring day in 1941. By this time, I weighed only 50 kilogrammes, about 25 kilogrammes below what I had weighed at the beginning of the war. I was practically what we called in camp parlance a Musselmann, at least physically, because my body was literally skin and bones and could not survive much longer, or so it seemed. I always hoped for a good work assignment, but my heart fell when I saw a prisoner approaching my Blockältester with request for some prisoners for his work group – it was one of the SK foremen. My hopes disappeared because I knew I had no chance to survive that day working with the SK. With no fat on my body, there was nothing to protect my bones from the inevitable blows of the foreman's club. I also knew that this would be heavy manual labour, because the SK was engaged in constructing houses for the SS officers. My body was simply not up to the work and I was certain I was lost.

The construction site was very close to the main camp, so it took us about ten minutes to march there. Once there, I was pleasantly surprised that I was not assigned to transport sand using the narrow gauge rail – I knew that I would be dead by the end of that day if I had had to run with the rail carts. Instead, I was ordered to join the line of prisoners who were moving the excavated soil from the construction site to the nearest rail line. Instead of using machinery or heavy equipment to move the soil, the SS used slave labour to shift it, using spades. The excavated soil was piled beside the site and the prisoners would form a chain. Prisoners at the initial pile, using their shovels, would shift that pile two metres toward the rail line, creating a second pile of sand. Another team of prisoners would shift the second pile another two metres toward the rail line, until there was a line of piles of sand, slowly moving away from the excavation and to the railcars. About fifteen prisoners were involved in this process. I was in the middle of the chain. It was relatively easy work, the soil was dry, loose sand, so easy to lift. My objective was to ensure that the pile I was moving did not get depleted visibly, and the pile to which I was moving the sand was not growing excessively. It was a warm, sunny day, and I began to hope that I might even survive the day.

Unfortunately, I forgot about the foreman. The SK foreman was working his way down the line, 'encouraging' us to work. His method of encouragement was simple. He carried a heavy oak club, about ten centimetres thick and two metres long, which he wielded with two hands. He started with the first prisoner in the line, standing behind him, about one metre to the left. He lifted his club above his head and dropped it on the prisoner's back. Then he moved on and did the same to the next prisoner in the line. His face registered no emotion – evidently, this was routine. Very soon he was behind me.

I did not want to die in such a stupid manner. I could not avoid being hit and I could not control the velocity of the club hitting my back. However, I could influence the force with which the club would hit me - that much I knew, based on the laws of physics I had studied in school. Thus, I could prevent the foreman's club from breaking my bones, provided that I correctly estimated the moment when the club hit my body. Just as the club fell upon my back, I collapsed the upper part of my body and relaxed all my muscles. It worked! The club pushed my body forward, but no bones were broken. And the foreman moved on to the next prisoner. Some of the prisoners in the line fell when they were struck, but nobody appeared to be terminally hurt.

The most deadly task for this Kommando was moving the sand to a distant part of the construction site using the rail carts. The carts consisted of an open steel box, about one cubic metre in volume and on four small wheels, that could be tipped to dump its load. You also carried a two-metre pole as well, which you used to heave the cart back on the tracks when it derailed. It did that frequently, as the tracks were not straight and the ground was uneven. The cart would be brought to the loading place and two prisoners, not the wagon crew, loaded the sand into the container, allowing the wagon crew a half-minute of rest. When the wagon was full of sand, the crew started moving.

This was very common procedure in the camp and used on a number of sites. However, there were some major differences between the technique of transportation used by the regular Kommando in the KZ and the technique used in the SK. Regularly, the crew consisted of four prisoners – in the SK it consisted of three prisoners. Regularly, the crew walked, quite rapidly, when the wagon was full of sand and ran when the wagon was empty. In the SK, the crew ran, whether the wagon was empty or full. In the regular Kommando, when one of the crew members was injured or died, he was replaced, so that the number of prisoners per cart was always four. In the SK, it was different. A crew member who was killed or died remained with the cart and had to be transported with the sand. Thus, after the sand had been loaded, his corpse would be put on top of the sand in the wagon and hauled along with the sand. This made the loading and unloading procedure much more complicated. After running to their destination, the remaining two crewmembers first had to unload the corpse, then the sand, reorient the cart, reload the corpse and run back for the next load of sand, where they would have to repeat the whole process. Any derailment when running to and fro was a calamity. With a corpse in the wagon, it was even worse. Two men could lift an empty wagon, even with a corpse inside, and put it back on the rail; however, the task was extremely difficult when the wagon is full of sand, with a corpse on top. The death of one crew member usually meant the extermination of the whole team.

The work was hard, but I tried to make my efforts as efficient as possible, minimizing the expenditure of energy. I became an automaton, moving sand. For a short moment, I recalled Captain Tadeusz Tazber, my commanding officer in the school for reserve officers. He had insisted that officers had to be able to withstand much more physical hardship than the common soldiers and had put us through a very harsh, rigorous kind of boot camp. I think that prisoners with some military background were at an advantage. They were used to obeying apparently meaningless and harsh orders from their military training. At that time I had heartily resented the primitive hardship he had imposed, but now I was grateful – it was helping me to stay alive. Nonetheless, while I was momentarily safe, because the foreman, having beaten the prisoners once, seemed satisfied with our production rate and so had refrained from beating us again, it was certain it would not last. I was concerned that Bugdalle would visit the construction site. I already had seen Bugdalle in action and it seemed that no one in the camp could surpass his brutality. Since he had not made it to the site that morning, the odds were good that he would visit that afternoon.

When noon arrived, our Kommando returned to the camp for the noon meal – the usual bowl of soup. After the meal, I approached our Blockältester and asked him not to send me back to the SK Kommando. At that time my German was still broken, but I succeeded in conveying to him my fear that I would not survive another six hours in the SK and that I would like to see my mother again before I died. He smiled and reassigned me. That afternoon, I worked in one of many work crews where no particular skill was required, but the killing rate was low. I am still grateful to my Blockältester for letting me stay alive.

Soon, I moved to another Kommando, the Pumpenhaus. By that time, I had learned how to change my Kommandos, an important thing. Typically, there was much movement between Kommandos, as each always needed extra labour. What you did was find out which Kommandos needed additional labour and volunteer for the good ones as fast as possible, by asking your Blockältester to transfer you. Initially, the rumour was that the foreman of the Pumpenhaus was beating the prisoners under his command. This was true, in a way. His Bauführer, who was an SS officer, believed that corporal punishment should be applied as frequently as possible and on any pretext. The foreman could not, of course, refuse to obey such an order. So what he did was temper his beatings. For example, if you beat someone with a board, you can hit them with the thin edge, which makes very little noise but is very painful. Or you can hit them with the wide edge, which is very noisy but much less painful. And that is what he did – so he obeyed the orders, but mitigated the damage. So when I found that out, I arranged to be transferred to the Pumpenhaus. That was a good Kommando. It is where I learned the building trade (this helped me afterwards, when I began designing) – how to mix and pour concrete, how to bend reinforcing rods, how to carry bricks up a ladder and how to lay brick. Nobody was killed during the few weeks I was in this Kommando, nobody was harmed. No bones were broken, no blood was shed. And that is where I learned the words to "It's a long way to Tipperary" from one of the other prisoners with whom I was working. I got to know a few of the other prisoners, such as Tolek and Waclaw Plonski. It was Waclaw who taught us the song. We became very close and supported each other through everything. At one point, later, Waclaw became ill. He had a stomach problem, but because he didn't have a fever, he didn't qualify to go to the hospital. He couldn't eat the soup we got each day, so he gave his soup to the two of us, in exchange for one of our rations of bread. Still, Waclaw got weaker and weaker. At one point, when he got really bad, I carried him to the Apellplatz, because he had to attend evening roll call. If you didn't attend roll call, you were executed immediately. So you struggled to roll call no matter what. He died in December 1940. Many in the Kommandos did.

I remember one other Kommando, it was much more difficult. It was in March 1941, because I can remember that my shoes were sodden from the ice and snow. I was working at a brick kiln, carrying bricks from the furnace and stacking them outside the building. The change in temperatures, from a scalding 80 degrees Celsius by the furnace to the ice cold of outside, was very difficult. It was very hard and heavy work, and very hard on the hands because we had no gloves and the bricks were so hot, they took the skin off your palms. But at least it was better work than running with trees and nobody was hitting me. So the chance of survival was better here.

Each day was a struggle to survive. One slip could cost a prisoner his life. And yet, there were moments of humanity and kindness that threw the rest of the hell that was life in the concentration camp into stark relief. One such moment happened during the summer of 1941.

It was a warm and sunny summer day, but I was tired and cold. We had started working at 5 o'clock in the morning and there were still about five hours left to the workday. I just could not get warm. Working harder would have warmed me up, but it would have sapped my strength, and I did not think I would survive the day if I let that happen. My resources were very thin by this point in my imprisonment. In addition, I had had two cases of very bad luck that day. The first case was due to my own mistake. The second was a consequence of the first.

The whole day was an unusual one - for the first time since I had arrived at Sachsenhausen, I was assigned to a Kommando that was working in Oranienburg, a small city not far from the camp and not far from Berlin. We were building a sewer system in a residential area of the city. I was in shock, just from seeing the city. It was a typical residential neighbourhood, of single-family homes with neat lawns, small flower gardens, and with normal, properly dressed men and women walking along the sidewalks, and children playing in the yards. It was like a fairy tale, so far removed was it from what had become my reality. To make it seem even more unreal, the foreman's and the SS guards' behaviour had changed markedly. There was no shouting, no threats, no beating, not even a raised voice. True, I could sense that these people, the residents, were very uncomfortable around us. We did not belong, we felt that as well. We were intruding and not welcome, our presence was dangerous and only just tolerated. Some viewed us with contempt, some with open hostility. I also saw embarrassment and confusion in the faces of some who passed by. I suppose we did not look like the hardened criminals they had been told we were.

Because I knew nothing about constructing sewer systems, I was given heavy, physical labour. Digging the ditches for the pipe was considered more responsible work, because if it was not done properly, the walls of the ditches could collapse. So instead, I was assigned to transporting the concrete sewer pipe from the storage area to the ditch. The pipe was big, about one metre in diameter, and very heavy and awkward to move. We used steel rollers to move it. I had to be very careful in pacing myself. If I worked too quickly, I would deplete my resources and literally kill myself. If I worked too slowly, I would be labelled a lazy worker, with just as disastrous consequences - although the punishment would be delayed until we returned to the camp at the end of the day. This meant that I had to watch very carefully for the foreman and for the SS guards, who were looking for any signs of flagging. And my attention wandered from the work that I was doing, and the end of one of the rollers we used to move the pipe ran over my left big toe and crushed it. The pain was excruciating and my dilemma was immediate.

I could report the injury to the foreman, but I didn't know him or how he would react. I was also of no consequence in the camp hierarchy - I was a relatively 'young' prisoner, with a high number, and with no influential friends and nothing with which to bribe him. He could easily accuse me of having done it on purpose, to get out of working. This often happened. The results were not pretty. If accused this way, the prisoner was interrogated, and one usually died from such an interrogation or, if the prisoner confessed, he was condemned to death. Alternatively, I could try to hide my injury and hope that it would not visibly impair my ability to work, walk and run. At the end of the day, back in the camp, I could appeal to my Blockältester for help. Or I could wait a few days, to see how the injury healed, before approaching him. I decided to not tell anyone.

Then my second case of bad luck happened. I was running back to the storage area, as we were required to do, and another prisoner noticed that I ran in an odd way because of the injury. I had noticed that he had looked at me in a strange way, several times. Then this prisoner approached the SS guard and, with cap in hand, pointed me out to the guard, explaining what he had seen. I could not believe it - one prisoner denouncing another! The man had to be insane! When the word of what he had done got out in the camp, he would be dead and it would be a very painful death. The SS officer was visibly embarrassed. He refused to make a decision on the matter himself, and called over the foreman. The three of them talked for a short while and the prisoner was dismissed. The guard gave me a long look and then dismissed the foreman as well. The foreman strolled up to me and noted my number. I was numb. I was furious with myself because I couldn't think of a way out of the situation. So I waited for him to record my number and, thus, begin the process. Instead, the foreman looked at me, told me to be careful and walked away. I was shocked and bewildered. At least for now, I was safe. I returned to the storage area to pick up another piece of pipe.

Over the course of the day, I had a chance to observe the young man who had denounced me. He was in his twenties, about my age, but he looked much older, as did we all. His face was contorted with terror and fear. His number and tag identified him as a Jew who had only recently arrived at the camp. It was clear that he had succumbed to the atmosphere of terror created by the SS and did not have the strength of character to withstand the psychological and physical torment inflicted on him. This is why he had denounced me, because he thought he could save his own life in doing so. He did not realize that it would make no difference.

So I continued to move pipe and tried not to dwell on my bad luck, although not very successfully. And then a bizarre thing happened, that again upset all my assumptions. A woman kept peering out of the door of one of the houses we passed as we moved between the ditches and the storage area. I got the impression she was both looking at the prisoners, but also trying to figure out where the foreman and the SS were. And then, the door opened wide, and a small girl appeared in the doorway. She was dressed very neatly and about six or seven years old. She had an apron on, over her dress, and she held the corners of the apron firmly in both of her tiny hands, making a pocket out of it. Whatever she had in the apron was bulky and heavy, because she was making a visible effort not to spill the contents. Both she and her mother who stood behind her were looking around attentively, seeming to wait for the right moment, whatever that was. It was such strange behaviour that I couldn't stop watching them. I glanced at the foreman, who was clearly very tense and gave the appearance of concentrating furiously on the sewage line. Then the SS guard turned and walked away from that part of the site.

Suddenly, the door opened further and the small girl ran from the house to the sidewalk, holding her apron tightly. She stopped on the sidewalk, looked to the right and the left to see if anyone was watching her, then stepped up to the edge of the ditch where the prisoners were installing the pipe. She let go of her apron. Apples - early summer, light green apples - tumbled down into the ditch. She turned around and ran back into the house and disappeared through the door that closed quietly behind her. My breath was taken away. The miracle was over.

There were not many apples and so I did not get one, but that was not important. The compassion of the woman and child gave me hope, once again. We were not alone. Their action was a defence of human dignity, and they were fighters, as we were. She was German and she was free, but she was one of us.

Pindera reached his personal nadir on the night of Friday, 13 February 1942. That night is seared into his memory, for good reason.

The night was beautiful. Not a single cloud obscured the dark blue sky. I could clearly see the Great Dipper and, looking past the North Star, my favourite constellation, the Cassiopeia. Even the sharp glare of the searchlights regularly sweeping over the ten thousand men silently standing on the Appellplatz could not obscure this wonderful view, the enchantment of the deep winter sky filled with brilliant stars.

There was little snow on the Apellplatz; no snow can survive having several thousand feet trampling over it. The soil was frozen hard, and rang whenever the men moved. In the Dead Zone, the space between the barbed wire and the electrified fence which encircled the camp, the snow was unmarked and sparkled in the light of the searchlights, as they swept past. The cold was piercing, the temperature was at least twenty degrees Celsius below zero. The cold and the tension in the atmosphere killed any feeling of hunger I might have had, and suspended any sense of time. Each second seemed an eternity. Time seemed as frozen and still as the immobile men standing at attention in the Apellplatz. Ten thousand of us, standing quiet and obedient, with machine guns trained on us. I glanced at the huge, illuminated clock on the watchtower - it was 11:23 p.m. We had been standing there for just one hour and twenty-three minutes past our usual curfew, but it seemed as if we had been there for an eternity. Almost six hours earlier, the Blockführers had received the head counts from the Blockältesters, and every prisoner had long been accounted for. Still, we were held in formation, for we were being punished. It must have been an awesome sight from the watchtower, fifty blocks of prisoners, some two or three hundred each, standing at rigid attention in formation, five rows deep, perfectly still, expressionless, guarded by just a few dozen, a handful, of SS and Blockführers, who held in their hands the power over life and death for these ten thousand prisoners.

Walking up and down between the rows were the Blockführers, looking for the slightest breach of discipline, even just a turn of the head or a movement of the hand. Any such movement meant instant death. It was even too dangerous to glance at the reason for the punishment: the burned-out structure in the first circle of barracks, just behind my back. To exchange a word with one of my neighbours in the row would have been fatal. All I could do was to look at the clock above the machine guns, or to move my eyes slowly to the right or to the left, without changing the expression on my face. And to think. I had become used to the bestial and perverse cruelty of the SS. I had learned to conquer fear, terror and panic. Over the past year, I had taught myself how to stay alive in the midst of death and random execution. I had learned how to manage the demands made on my increasingly weakened body, without appearing to be slow in the heavy physical tasks I had been assigned. I had decided to be one of the last men to die, and to live long enough to be able to fight back. Still, this night shook me to the core. The stillness around me, the menacing silence, broken only by the quiet commands of the guards, directing the teams collecting the corpses, or their short laughs when they dispatched dying men, was filled with doom, and I began to sink into despair. The night had already lasted too long. Midnight came - and went. And time stopped again. And men began to give up and they began to die. The teams of corpse bearers became very busy, and they were now required not only to run when returning from the mortuary, but also to run there.

I, too, was starting to feel the bitter cold. I am six feet tall and that meant I was standing in the last row of my column, with my back exposed directly to the frigid air. Worse yet, my back was also exposed to the careful inspection of the Blockführers as they strolled among the prisoners. My body temperature, which was already low, began to drop more rapidly, and there was little I could do about it, standing at attention and forbidden to move a muscle. Even minor calesthenics, like rotating my shoulder-blades (which required very little movement and could be done when there were no guards nearby), were less and less effective. My body weight, by this time, had dropped from seventy-five kilogrammes to forty. I had very little body fat left, and depleted muscle tissue is a poor source of warmth. The clothing I was wearing was little protection against the elements - a shirt and pants made of a thin hempen fabric. I was already worn out from a particularly harsh work assignment, which had killed ten men just that day.

The weather changed after midnight. Thin, low clouds covered the stars, a light snow began to fall, and gusts of wind swept the Apellplatz. We could smell the smoky, wet timber from the burned-out barrack; then the repulsive, sweet smell of burning human flesh from the crematorium. The scene had become otherworldly - the odours, the slowly falling flakes of snow, caught in the sweeping beams of light, the thousands of grim, mute, immobile men dressed in striped uniforms with numbers on their left breasts and right legs, the randomly scattered bodies of dead or dying men lying where they dropped to the ground, the teams of corpse bearers running to and fro, the SS walking leisurely and alertly between the columns, the unearthly stillness broken from time to time by the quiet, sinister voices of the guards, the whole scene partially obscured by the fog-like snow.

By one o'clock in the morning, I had lost all hope that we would be allowed some rest in our barracks before reveille at five o'clock. I was not sure any more that I would be able to stay on my feet until then, but I began to fear that we would be expected to. Looking for anything that could give me some strength, I tried to compare the condition of the men in my column, many of whom were friends of mine, with the condition of others in columns nearby. As I expected, we seemed much better off than the others. Our column consisted, for the most part, of young, strong army reserve officers and privates. They were the soldiers of a beaten, but not defeated army who had decided against going to the prisoner-of-war camps, but had tried to escape to join their units abroad and then were caught, like me. The others were Polish university and high school students, members of the intelligensia, workers, peasants, all of whom had been brought up in a close-knit society which revered strength of character, independent thinking and a sense of duty. Each one of us was intensely patriotic, and grimly determined to stay alive until the first chance to inflict damage upon the despised enemy. So the rate of dying in my column seemed to be less severe than it was in other columns.

After midnight, there was another unsettling change. Earlier, the men who died had fallen to the frozen ground before they were actually dead. Once fallen, they died quietly or were quickly dispatched by the passing guards. Now, the men were dying quietly on their feet, not falling to the ground until they were already dead. Occasionally, I was certain I saw disappointment on the faces of some of the SS, robbed of the pleasure of killing a fallen man. Bizarrely, a fragment of conversation from years and worlds ago flickered across the jumbled thoughts in my head. Back in Warsaw, a friend and I had debated the necessity of, in this skeptical, but enlightened twentieth century, developing one's character over one's intellect and moral principles. I finally knew the answer, but had no one to tell.

I looked at the clock again - it was one-thirty. The night had become interminable. Very suddenly, I had a crawling feeling that someone desperately wanted my attention. Quite involuntarily my eyes moved slowly to the left and stopped at the face of my neighbour in the row. His face was white, his eyes opened wide and he was looking at me intensely. I glanced at his serial number. He was a German, a political prisoner and had been in the camp only a few months longer than I. I knew nothing about him. As we locked eyes, his expression slipped to one of resignation. I whispered, without moving my lips, "Don't...", but it was to no avail. He closed his eyes and an expression of surrender swept his face. Suddenly he collapsed, slightly backward, falling on his left side. Feelings of pity and weakness overwhelmed me. He was not much older than I.

Very soon, I heard the relaxed, strong and confident steps of an SS officer moving in my direction. The steps stopped where my companion had fallen. I could not see the face of the officer and to look up and into his face would have been a serious breach of discipline. All I could see was my fallen companion and the officer's boots. The boots were spotless and elegant. My companion lay still, apparently dead. After a few seconds, one of the boots lifted from the ground and kicked him in the chest. It was a clean, standard kick to the heart. My companion lifted his head slightly, sighed and said, in a quiet, resigned voice, "Let me die."

I could not turn my eyes away, although I was certain I was about to witness yet another senseless murder of a fallen prisoner. To my surprise, I was wrong. The boot hung in the air for a few seconds and then slowly, resolutely returned to the ground. Both I and the boots watched my companion die, with his gaze turned serenely to the sky. After how many minutes, I thought I heard the officer sigh. A sigh of relief? Of compassion? Of resignation? I don't know, but the boots then moved away. I was puzzled, shocked. This was not typical behaviour for the SS. He had let the prisoner die a natural death, instead of finishing the job. An inconceivable thought entered my mind - was it possible that the SS were not so monolithically barbarian as they appeared? Was it possible that there were some human beings among them?

At that moment, I remember feeling a powerful change overcome me. I became angry and drew strength from that anger. I became convinced, determined that I would survive that night, as would my companions, and we would survive the next night, and the next. A thousand nights, until the final victory, our victory. We would win. My unknown German friend would not die in vain.

Nonetheless, the night took its toll on me. I grew more and more numb. Nothing mattered any more, except staying alive. While my spirit was strong, my body was being pushed past its limits. I was physically a Musselman, a name given to those whose bodies and spirits were damaged beyond repair by the conditions in the camp. With their loss of will, these prisoners lost any self-respect and as a result, became begging, scavenging animals. At that stage, they had only a few weeks left to live. They died of simple exhaustion - their bodies had no fat, their muscles atrophied, as well as their internal organs. Their movements were slow and visibly impaired, and their eyes, clouded over. They no longer had any pride. While my own will and self-respect were as strong as ever, my body did not obey me any longer and was visibly deteriorating. Whenever I sat, I felt pain where my buttocks used to be, and I could touch my spine from the front of my body, through my belly. There was nothing I could do about it. It was simply not possible to recover while performing heavy physical labour under a hostile winter sky, meagrely clothed, eating only nine hundred calories a day. That night almost killed me, yet somehow, I managed to persevere. I still don't know how.

Over time, the brutality lessened a bit, in relative terms. Pindera recalls an announcement made at evening roll call toward the end of 1941. Reichsminister Heinrich Himmler, chief of the SS, had ordered that any killing of prisoners or beating of prisoners that resulted in a prisoner's immediate death, had to follow a prescribed procedure as set out by his office. Indeed, Himmler's decree was easily circumvented. This directive was not a ban on killing prisoners, it was merely intended to reduce the random execution of prisoners. All that the SS guard had to do was 'construct' an incident in which the prisoner was forced to be insubordinate. Nonetheless, this was an important shift in the thinking of the SS. By the winter of 1941/1942, it was clear even to the Germans that the war was not going to end soon. The availability of labour increasingly came to be seen as an invaluable and exploitable resource. Himmler saw the worsening wartime situation as an opportunity to create a position of strength for the SS after the war, as well as influence the wartime economy, by making the camps a key source of forced labour. In early 1942, Himmler's chief economic advisor, Oswald Pohl, was urging Camp Commandants to regard the camps as primarily economic entities, not political. He was asking them to shift emphasis from the 're-education' of the prisoners to their economic exploitaiton. In March 1942, this new status was formalized when the camps were made subordinate to the SS Economic and Administrative Office headed by Pohl. There was growing concern among the leaders of the SS about the climbing mortality rates in the camps and what that was costing the SS in lost revenue. In December 1942, in a circular addressed to Camp Commandants, Himmler ordered that corporal punishment be used only as a last resort when all other forms of punishment failed. The Inspector of the Concentration Camps, Glücks, who was the director of the entire concentration camp system, instructed the Commandants to take steps to reduce the mortality rate in a directive issued on 20 January 1943. And from 1942 onwards, rewards were offered the prisoners for good work, which enabled prisoners to acquire tobacco and extra food. Indeed, in May 1943, Pohl established a special system of rewards for prisoners. Those who distinguished themselves by industry, vigilance, good conduct and special achievements at work were granted special privileges, such as additional food, money rewards, tobacco and permission to visit the brothel. And the SS began to train certain skilled workers among the prisoners.

None of these directives had much impact on the camps. Increased economic exploitation translated into longer hours and harsher discipline, with minimal improvements in living or working conditions. Rather than trying to make each prisoner more efficient, the SS chose to mobilize more prisoners, and increase productivity in that way.

There may have been a bit more food and fewer random beatings, but the conditions continued to be horrific and the mortality rate remained appalling. The food remained grossly insufficient both in quality and quantity. Furthermore, while random beatings declined in number, formal punishments, properly approved by the SS chain of command, rose in number.

The most common killing method was quite simple. An SS officer who had selected a prisoner to be killed, took the prisoner close to the Postenkette or Line of Guards, ordered the prisoner to give him his cap, threw the cap behind the Postenkette and ordered the prisoner to retrieve it. When the prisoner crossed the Postenkette to retrieve his cap he was shot by the guard because he was trying to escape. If the prisoner refused to cross the Postenkette, he was shot by the SS officer for insubordination.

There were other cases when a SS officer publicly ordered a political prisoner to do something that violated the ethical or moral principles of a prisoner, for example to make a false statement, to beat another prisoner or to kill another prisoner. When the prisoner refused to follow the order, there was no retreat for the prisoner or for the SS officer. For the prisoner, this was the matter of preserving his sense of principles and personal dignity, even at the cost of his life. The SS officer had no choice either, for he faced severe punishment himself if he permitted the prisoner's insubordination to go unpunished.

However, if the insubordination was manifested privately, occasionally the SS could choose to ignore it. Such was the case with Harry Naujoks, the first Lagerältester. In May 1942, he was called to the officer of the Lagerführer, SS-Hauptsturmführer Fritz Suhren, who ordered him to execute a criminal prisoner by hanging. Himmler himself had ordered that this hanging be performed not by a SS officer, but by a respected political prisoner. Harry refused and discussed this matter confidentially with a respected member of the leadership of the underground resistance organization in the camp, who supported Harry's decision to refuse this order, regardless of consequences. Two days later, after the morning roll call on Easter Sunday, Harry was ordered to take his place close to the gallows. It was a sunny spring day in 1942. The gallows were of a special kind, with a winch used to slowly raise the prisoner being executed by a rope wrapped around his neck. It was a particularly slow, painful and grisly way to die. But Harry did not have to turn the winch, although he was forced to stand beside the gallows. Suhren chose, instead, as executioner, a young prisoner whose will had been broken by several weeks of cruel torture in the Bunker, a special building built for such purposes.

Sometimes the pseudo-legalistic mindset of the Nazis created bizarre circumstances. It was in the spring of either 1942 or 1943. We had gathered in the Appellplatz for morning roll call. A gallows had been erected in the centre of the square. After the end of the roll call, one Russian prisoner was called forward, led to the gallows and the noose was put around his neck. While the prisoner was being prepared for execution, the SS Rapportführer read the death sentence signed by the Reichsminister Heinrich Himmler. When the sentence was read, the Russian prisoner, with the rope still around his neck, protested, in a quiet and persuasive voice, that he was not the person sentenced to death by hanging because his birthdate was different from that of the accused. It turned out that a mistake had been made – the wrong prisoner had been put on the gallows. After a few, very long minutes, the Rapportführer made his decision. He ordered that the execution of the prisoner on the gallows proceed. Then he ordered that the correct prisoner be brought to the gallows, had Himmler's order read for the second time and ordered the second prisoner hanged. The corpses of both prisoners were put in the same coffin. It appeared that it was better to hang one innocent man than to admit that the SS could make a mistake.

The second case is one that I vividly remember. It was different. A prisoner had been sentenced to death for attempting to escape. In such cases, the execution was a complicated and long one. First, the sentenced prisoner had to walk across the Appellplatz and shout "I hail you, I (the name), I am here again." Afterwards, the prisoner was bound to a frame and received fifty lashes on the buttocks with a whip that was designed to slash the skin, and he was kept conscious all the time. Of course, for all practical purposes he was dead already – I knew of no prisoner who received fifty lashes and survived. One could survive twenty-five, but not fifty. After fifty lashes, the prisoner was led to the gallows and hung in a more humane manner – by being dropped, not by being pulled up. In this particular case, however, when the trapdoor was released, the rope broke and the prisoner fell to the ground. The Appellplatz fell very quiet, as quiet as if it was completely empty. The tension was thick in the air, as twenty thousand prisoners waited to see what would happen next. I expected, as I suspect all the other prisoners did, that the prisoner would now be removed to the hospital, where he would be allowed to die quietly and painlessly. There is an old tradition that someone cannot be hanged twice for the same offence. We were wrong. After a few minutes of consideration, the Rapportführer ordered, in a firm voice, that the dying prisoner be hanged again. In the silence that accompanied this announcement, one brave Dutchman said out loud, in a voice everyone heard, what we all felt. "This is obscene." The words hung in the air. And, although both the prisoner and the Dutchman died, the latter hideously, we all were stronger for his bravery. He had proven that the power of the SS was limited - they could break our bodies, but not our spirit.

In spite of the brutality of the Kommandos, all prisoners at Sachsenhausen were entitled to certain privileges. One was that each prisoner was allowed to send one letter every two weeks to whomever they chose. The letter had to be brief, written on a form provided by the camp, and written in clear German, with simple sentences and no codes. There were restrictions on what the prisoners could say in their letters, and in each letter they had to state that they were happy and in good health. It was also a privilege that could be and was revoked easily - as punishment for some real or perceived misdemeanour. At the top of each form were strict instructions:

> Each prisoner may receive and send two letters or postcards in a month. Each letter [received] may not be more than four pages of 15 lines each in length and it must be clear and easily read. Packages are forbidden. Cash remittances are only permitted in the form of postal orders, which may only record the christian and surname, birthdate, and prisoner number, no other communication. Money, photos or any other inclusion in letters is forbidden...

Pindera used his bi-weekly letters to correspond with his mother, who saved all the letters he wrote her. The letters, although carefully phrased to avoid the wrath of the German censors and to avoid unduly alarming his mother, reveal much about life in the camp, and about what preoccupied Pindera while interned. These letters were an important lifeline for Pindera, a crucial link to an outside world that seemed increasingly remote. They were a source of news about his mother, stepfather and sister, Dani, however cryptic, as well as a source of much-needed moral support. The letters arrived as regularly as was possible considering they were being sent from Poland, an occupied territory subjected to a vicious Nazi regime, to a political prisoner in a concentration camp not far from Berlin. However, whenever there was a break in the flow, the panic was clear in Pindera's own letters.

> Dear Mother and Dani!
> I have waited so long for a letter but I have not had one since the last time, I am very concerned. Are you all right, Mother? Write! As quickly as possible, my mother - I wait with impatience. *(27 April 1941)*

And...

> Dear Mother and Dani!
> I was very unhappy because I have received no letter since the last time. Today I have received a letter written on 1 May. I was afraid you were sick. *(11 May 1941)*

When he didn't hear from his family, Pindera's imagination ran riot - he feared his mother had fallen ill, or worse. He was also concerned that the money they were sending him was leaving them short. Indeed, he was amply supported by his family and by a network of friends. As permitted by the regulations, beginning in October 1940, Pindera began to receive postal orders in Deutschmarks which were deposited to his account. The process of getting the money to him was a convoluted one, but it worked, and it made an important difference to his life, and thus ability to survive, in the camp. The money originally was funnelled into his account through a gentleman Pindera called Uncle Weslowski, in Berlin. The money was probably funneled through the Polish resistance. At the store, the prisoners could purchase a variety of essentials, and so the extra money was critical. Pindera explained...

With the money in the account, I could buy shoelaces, toothpaste, a toothbrush, the blank forms for letters and the stamps to mail them. Sometimes, I could buy a small piece of pumpernickel bread, but very seldom. It was also possible to buy a small tin of sweetened potato syrup, which I would eat very slowly on Sunday. It would take me two hours, because if you ate it too quickly, you could kill yourself. You see, my digestive system was so bad, it could not deal with so much at once.

Later on, the SS administration introduced a kind of wage for some selected prisoners who worked in various enterprises, in the form of camp money, called Prämienschein. When I worked for the Baubüro, I received four Marks per week. This money was equivalent to real Reichsmarks (RM) and could be spent as the prisoner wished, depending on what was available. Not all prisoners got Prämienschein, only those doing professional work. The amount of wages ranged from one RM to four RM weekly. Note that prisoners were leased to various companies and corporations for four to eight RM a day or more, depending on the kind of work being performed. I found out, once, that I was being charged out at two RM a day, for unskilled labour, but when I was in the Baubüro, I was charged out at more than 200RM monthly. The criminal prisoners usually spent their money to buy a fifteen-minute visit in the KZ brothel, which cost four RM. The political prisoners chose to boycott this brothel because the girls were selected by the SS administration from the women's concentration camps. Instead, I spent it on postal cards, stamps, shoe polish, soap, toothpaste and toothbrushes, and on rare occasions, on jam, syrup or bread, when it was available. Everything had to be purchased in the camp canteen and charged against my account. I was forbidden to own any amount of cash.

It appears, from the references in the letters that Pindera received approximately 30DM each month, although it seems that there may have been a period of time during the summer of 1941 when the funds dried up. Pindera had stopped thanking his mother for the postal orders in the letters he wrote during that time (otherwise, he was diligent in thanking her and accounting for each postal order received). And in his letter home, dated 28 September 1941, his concern for his mother's welfare was palpable...

Dear loved ones!
Thank you for your letter of 16 September, which I received on the 22nd. I am very heartsick that you have such difficult living and working conditions, couldn't you, Dana, get lighter work? I suggest that my Mother sell my officer's cavalry dress boots and the breeches, and that would give her some money. Do not buy me a sweater, because I can buy one cheaper.... Here, as always, I think of you constantly. It grieves me that I cannot help you. I have the greatest hope that this will end, and we will all be together.... Your Jerzy.

Both suggestions were sound ones, as the riding boots and breeches would get a good price and Pindera could, indeed, 'organize' a sweater cheaply in the camp - from Kanada. It was strictly against the regulations, but that kind of barter was common.

Although the instructions on the form for the letters indicated that parcels were forbidden, packages were getting into the camp. In October 1940, Pindera wrote his mother in early October 1940 to tell her that another prisoner, Lolek, had received some sweaters, among other things, and that she should contact his family and find out how they arranged it. As early as mid-November 1940, Pindera was telling his mother that he was receiving parcels from Berlin and Lublin. Very soon, he was receiving both food and clothing from both family and friends. The parcels came very sporadically, but each one was received with profound gratitude. He received two in November 1940, from connections in Berlin and Lublin; a special thin white bread, part of a Polish Christmas tradition, in December 1940; another 'great package' in January 1941; and winter-weight underwear in January 1942. In 1943, this restriction was lifted and parcels were permitted. From that point on, the flow of parcels became more regular. The prisoners believed rightly that the change in policy was because their labour had become more valuable. Whatever the reason, the parcels were important to a prisoner's survival.

Another thread that wove itself through his correspondence with his mother and sister was concern for his stepfather, who had gone missing. As early as 29 September 1940, Pindera began to ask for news about him. His stepfather had had to flee, when Poland was invaded. He had worked in the political division of the county administration, and was involved somehow in monitoring and dealing with the various Ukrainian and German nationalist movements, as well as the communists. This had put him in a very dangerous position when the Soviet Union invaded Chelm. The family knew, even before Pindera was captured, that he had escaped and gone to Lvov, but that was all the family knew. It was not until after the war that they learned he had been captured by and died at the hands of the Soviets.

Initially, in September 1940, Pindera was hopeful, at least in his correspondence with his mother, that liberation would come soon. Meanwhile, his mother was busily trying to work for his release. In September 1940, she had heard about a Gestapo officer in Chelm who was able to arrange the release of prisoners for the right price. Unfortunately, he was caught before Mrs. Pindera could connect with him.

There was another possible avenue of escape that Pindera wanted his mother to pursue. His stepfather had been born in what had become the Russian part of Poland, and Pindera hoped that meant his stepfather was now a Soviet citizen. If that was the case, perhaps he could then claim Soviet citizenship, and in that way, escape the camp. At that time, the Soviet Union and the Third Reich were still friendly and such an exchange might be possible, or so he hoped. The wheels ground slowly however. In early March 1941, he asked his mother,

> Can Tadek [meaning himself] receive his father's citizenship? I think that Father's citizenship association [i.e. potential Russian citizenship] could facilitate the management. (*2 March 1941*)

Later that month, he evidently got a reply from his mother, but it was not to his liking. On 30 March, he wrote tersely,

> Dear Mother and Dani!
> I received your letter of 13 March on 20 March. ... I insist, you should not go through with the possibility. Tadzio has no German citizenship. I know for certain he has Russian citizenship. (*30 March 1941*)

Over the course of his letters home, Pindera had created a means of passing on news about himself that would have been forbidden if he had been open about it. He created a brother, Tadek or Tadzio, who he put in a prisoner-of-war camp, and then reported to his mother what Tadek, who was really himself, wrote to him. In this way, when he spoke of Tadek or Tadzio, he was really communicating information about himself. Apparently his mother had proposed an alternate way of getting Pindera out of the camp - he could claim German citizenship. One of his university friends had done just that. His friend's uncle was Volksdeutsch, of Germanic origin, and that gave the uncle German citizenship. The uncle adopted Pindera's friend who then immediately gained German citizenship himself, and was even able to continue his studies at the Technical University of Vienna. Pindera's birth father was an Austrian citizen and so, technically, Pindera was an Austrian citizen. Austria had been absorbed into the Third Reich in 1938, which meant that he could potentially claim German citizenship. His mother apparently had asked him if he wished to renew that citizenship. He resolutely refused to consider that option in the letter dated 30 March 1941. He explained...

I could not look in the mirror at myself [if I did that] and
my colleagues in the KZ would have considered me a kind
of dirt.

On 13 April 1941, he reaffirmed his determination, when he wrote,

I think always about the second father. In no way should
you activate the affair of the first father.

*It all came to naught, and after the German invasion of the Soviet
Union, the discussion of citizenship disappears from the letters and
there is no more talk of getting out of the camps before the war's end.*

*Increasingly, Pindera pleaded for news from home, but not just
about the family. He was also keen for news about the war. Even before
22 June 1941, when Germany invaded the USSR, it appears that the
prisoners had heard rumours, because in late May 1941 and again in
mid-June of the same year, Pindera asked his mother for news about
his communist friend, Wladek, and his friends. This was another layer
of double-talk introduced - 'Wladek and friends' became synonomous
with the Soviet Union. The prisoners heard some news about the war's
progress, but it was scanty, so anything his mother could tell him would
be a bonus. In August of 1941, he was hopeful that the USSR would win
the war, and quickly. However, by September, he was losing hope that
the war would be over soon. As he wrote his mother...*

I am also heartsick that Tadek cannot help at all with the
poor colleagues of Wladek. It pleases me that he is able to
help himself.

*So Pindera knew that the Soviet Union was able to slow down the
German advance, but that the Allies were not going to come to the
USSR's aid soon. His letters are full of veiled requests for information
about the war's progress.*

*Through his letters, he also used his mother as a conduit for
information about his colleagues in the camp, asking her to pass on
information to their families. It was all done carefully and indirectly.
The 'code' as Pindera called it, was a kind of 'talking between the
lines'. In order to let a family know that their relative was alive and in
the camp, he would ask his mother to send his warmest greetings to
Frau Helena Chwedczak, for example, living in Ruda Opelier, and to
tell her that he was pleased that Josef was such a help to her. Or, to*

ask Mr and Mrs Kozinilisey whether Juska Linbutkowskie's apartment in Warsaw was in order. The problem for these prisoners was that their families had moved on, due to the war, so they did not know how to find them to send them a letter. Pindera's mother was involved with the Polish Red Cross and so had the means of tracking down the itinerant families.

One of the perhaps more surprising rights the prisoners had was to medical treatment. Of course, it was not available to all nor was it available for all injuries. As Pindera wrote...

Serious physical consequences of a random or of a purposeful beating were not considered an illness, even when the prisoner needed medical care. Such a prisoner was expected to live or die unassisted and, if he did not recover quickly, or his dying took too long, he was often helped to die. Furthermore, an illness was not considered legitimate when there was no elevated body temperature and when the prisoner could stand unsupported, even when he could not walk. In practice, on the other hand, any illness was considered legitimate when the body temperature exceeded 39 degrees Celsius. Even more unbelievable, in certain instances, National Socialist labour law applied, even within the barbed wire of the camp. For example, prisoners who were victims of work accidents were protected by the National Socialist labor law and were treated in the same manner as free German citizens. I remember one prisoner, who worked in the automotive depot, suffered an eye injury requiring surgery. Since there was no eye surgeon in the camp, that prisoner was transported by ambulance to an eye clinic in Berlin where a well-known specialist performed the surgery and saved the prisoner's eye. After his return to the KZ, that prisoner could be randomly killed, but that was an entirely different matter. It was a law that I took advantage of several times over the course of my stay at Sachsenhausen.

Part Three

The Baubüro

By February 1942, it was clear to Pindera that he was soon going to die. That fateful night in the Appellplatz, when he watched men collapse and die around him seemed to be the beginning of the end. He expected he had about two or three weeks more to live. He had become a walking skeleton. Although his spirit was not broken, his body had been weakened almost beyond repair, and there was nothing he could do to prevent what seemed certainly inevitable. While he tried to maintain his dignity at all times, he knew it was just a matter of time before his body would give out on him. It was the worst moment of his internment. And then something happened which turned his life around....

One of my younger colleagues, who somehow had won employment in the Baubüro or Construction Office in the camp, told me that they were looking for an engineer for the office. The Czech engineers who had been employed there had been released from the camp and, mistakenly, the other engineers in the camp had been killed. So there was no other engineer available in the camp. My colleague promised to draw the attention of the Baubüro's foreman to my existence. Perhaps, he hinted, it would be possible to arrange something. The next day, he found me and told me that Richard Adler, the foreman, wanted to see me. So I went to Adler's block. Adler was another political prisoner, a social democrat. He had become the foreman of the Baubüro because he was a trained construction technician. He knew the job, but was not an engineer, which is why he needed someone like me. He was the first Prominent I met.

The Prominenten were a particular class of prisoners. They were largely political prisoners, and they were the elite and leadership within the prisoner community. They held the most important positions within the prisoner administration and enjoyed certain privileges as a result. They also led the resistance in the camp.

When I saw his block, I was shocked! It was clean, neat. Rather than linoleum on the floor, it was polished wood. The tables and benches were nicely polished as well and varnished, rather than made of rough wooden boards like the tables and benches in my block. The walls were painted and clean, as well. And people spoke in low, even tones. The Blockältester, when he met me, greeted me very civily. I could not believe my eyes.

Then Adler gave me a test to determine my abilities. On the table, there was some paper and a pencil which I was given to use, so that I could answer the questions posed. The test was of my engineering skills and it lasted about one hour. At the end of the hour, it appeared I had passed the exam, because Adler told me, "Well, I am satisfied, but the Baubüro's SS manager (or Bauleiter) must decide." At that, my heart fell, I had no hope. I was convinced that I would not get the job, nor did it seem anything could save me from what seemed certain death. And I returned to my block.

Then two days later, during morning coffee, the Blockältester called my name and number. He told me that, after the morning roll call on the Appellplatz, I was to report to the Baubüro! I was astonished - the Baubüro was on another planet, as far as I was concerned. The one glimpse I had had of that world was on one very cold, wet, miserable day when we were being marched past its windows. I remember looking in the windows, and seeing prisoners in clean uniforms, drafting tables, desks, books... BOOKS! These had become an impossible dream. And so the Baubüro seemed like an enchanted land for me, in my misery and danger. And now I was being told to report there. That meant that Adler had somehow managed to 'arrange' my employment, in spite of my sentence. It appeared that the Gestapo could be persuaded to bend their rules on occasion - as my sentence had condemned me to outside work until death.

You must understand what the Baubüro was, in order to understand the opportunity I was being given. The Baubüro was the Civil Engineering Construction Office of the SS enterprise called the Bauleitung Nord der Waffen-SS und Polizei. This was a subsidiary of a powerful parent company, the Zentralbauleitung der Waffen-SS und Polizei, Berlin, which had its headquarters located in Oranienburg. The Zentralbauleitung was responsible for all the civil engineering projects of the various enterprises of the Waffen SS, including the concentration camps. This office designed and built all the buildings and infrastructure required by the Waffen SS, using the inmates of the concentration camps as cheap slave labour. The Bauleitung's labour needs even took precedence over other leading industrial corporations, such as the Heinkelwerke in Germensdorf or the Messerschmittwerke in Ausburg. There were two divisions in the Baubüro, a financial division responsible for cost evaluation and tracking the accounts related for the construction projects and the technical division responsible for the actual design and construction.

These enterprises, including the Bauleitung, leased prisoners from the camps for ten or twelve hours of labour a day, with the exception of Sundays. They typically were paid between two to four Reichsmarks daily per prisoner. This was extremely profitable for the camps, for the cost of maintaining the camps worked out to be approximately one Reichsmark a day per prisoner.

The Bauleitung was engaged in a wide variety of projects, including both labour-intensive and knowledge-intensive tasks. It was the Bauleitung that was responsible for the work assigned to the various Speerkommandos - the heavy, brutish, killing physical labour to which we prisoners were subjected - hauling trees, shifting sand, digging trenches, carrying bricks. The knowledge-intensive tasks were very different. They were design projects that ranged from the simple, such as designing a ladder for the side of the gas chambers to allow the delivery of special gas canisters to the roof of the chambers; to the complex, such as designing housing subdivisions, specialized factory buildings, special bunkers that could survive bombing raids. I had already been exposed, too much, to the first type of project - the labour-intensive ones. They were what had reduced me to my grossly depleted state. The Baubüro was engaged in the latter type of projects. And I was being ordered to be a part of them!

So I reported to the Baubüro. I remember that day very well. After roll call, I joined the Kommando Baubüro on the Appellplatz and we marched into the Industriehof where the Baubüro was located. It was in a special area of the camp, fenced off from the rest of the camp. I was the last one to enter the room. I came to a halt at the door and could not take another step. I could not believe my eyes. It had to be impossible, a bad dream, a dream that would weaken me. I saw a large, well lit and well heated room, with a clean bright floor, desks with drafting tables at their sides, typewriters, calculating machines, books. Books! It was unbelievable, I had to be hallucinating. The prisoners who had entered before me were removing their thin hemp jackets, revealing the usual blue-and-white striped uniforms, but their clothes were clean and in good repair. It was then I noticed that they were all wearing clean, warm leather shoes. Everybody was talking softly. No one raised their voices, there was not a sign of a stick with which to hit a prisoner. I felt as if I had suddenly been transported back in time from the only planet of any consequence to me, the KZ Sachsenhausen, to the Warsaw Technical University where I had studied. I could not help it - I felt tears in my eyes. It was only the second time that had happened (the first being when I saw the Soviet tanks roll into Luck). I also felt deeply, terribly embarrassed. My clothing was typical of a prisoner who had been performing hard physical work. My hands were red, swollen and covered in wounds and scars encrusted with dirt. My cheeks were sunken and my skin was grey. My shoes had wooden soles with leather tops and very noisy. I felt like a pariah.

I do not remember how long I stood in the door like that, afraid to move. After a while, I felt someone touch my arm. It was Richard Adler, who had finally noticed my embarrassment. He took me to a desk (my own desk!) and told me how to get writing material and how to get access to the books; showed me where the washroom was; explained how to respond to questions posed by SS officers; explained who was the boss, and what the functions were of the various SS officers I would encounter. I had a desk of my own, paper, pencils, drafting tools, a 22-digit calculating machine, a slide rule! I was dazed from the shock.

I don't remember much of what happened the rest of that day. I think I passed it in a haze. Nobody was shouting, nobody expected me to run, nobody hit me, nobody wanted to kill me. The room was warm, there was hot water in the washroom. Some even had family photographs on their desks. It was a paradise. One thing I do remember is the first project that Richard Adler assigned to me. I was to design reinforced concrete stairs for a large building. This was a bit of a surprise for me, as my training had been in aeronautical engineering, and I had only taken one survey course on the theory of structures, which had not discussed reinforced concrete. It was clear that I was going to have to learn the theory of reinforced concrete quickly, without letting anyone realize that I didn't know it already. Thankfully, I had learned something of it already, when I worked on the Kommando Pumpenhaus. Fortunately, too, the courses on mechanics and on airplane structures that I had taken at the Technical University of Warsaw had been very good and demanding, so I knew how to begin my project. I became immersed in the planning and was very surprised when Richard touched my arm and said it was time to go. I looked around and only then realized that everybody had already gone; Richard and I were the only ones left.

The next day, I was more relaxed and more confident. I was sure that I could master the necessary theory and perform satisfactorily. Ironically, the heavy manual labour I had had to perform in the previous two years had given me an extensive practical education in building technology. Unexpectedly, that experience proved invaluable now that I was in the Baubüro.

Within a few days, I had finished my first project. At that time, I worked alone and so did everything from designing the model for the calculation and estimation of dimensions, and the evaluation of stresses and deflections, to drafting the structural details and blueprints, and writing up the list of materials needed. Later, I would have working for me a team of two draftsmen, a specialist in materials specification and a typist. But that would take some time.

While this unexpected chance assured me of twelve hours of life every day, from six a.m. to six p.m., it did not solve my basic problem - that I was still literally dying of hunger. True, in the Kommando Baubüro, every prisoner received the Arbeitsportion or "work ration", a supplement allocated to those prisoners deemed especially important or to be rewarded. This work ration consisted of two one-centimetre thick slices of good dark bread, one of them covered in white margarine, with a thin piece of sausage between. This was, however, still too little, too late for me. My weight had dropped to forty kilograms and was still falling. About one week into my stint at the Baubüro, I realized that this was the end. Simply put, this wonderful opportunity to stay alive and perhaps even to fight back, had come too late. The realization came suddenly to me and I momentarily broke down. I could not control my face, nor could I talk, so I hid my face in my locker. As was the custom in the camps, no one said anything. This was a 'non-event', and the others ignored my momentary lapse, allowing me to recover with my dignity intact. A few minutes later, I was back in total control of myself, quiet and resigned.

The next day, at the Baubüro, before the noon break, one of the prisoners working in the financial division of the Baubüro, Georg Saur, came to my desk and invited me to his barrack right after I ate my noon soup. Georg was an old political prisoner, who had been in the camp for seven years. He was either a social democrat or a communist, I never knew for sure and it made no difference. He was a self-taught man, with an impressive knowledge of the philosophers, from Anaxagoras to the modern idealists and materialists. Georg did not explain why he had invited me and I did not ask, as was the custom in the camp. He only told me the number of his barrack, Block 4, which was a Prominentenblock, or barrack for the Prominent.

So, after finishing my dish of soup, I went to Block 4. The prisoners there looked entirely different from my colleagues in Block 16. They belonged to a small group who had survived extremely harsh treatment at the hands of the Gestapo and the SS. All of them were serving unlimited sentences for the crime of 'high treason', according to National Socialist law. Socially, they were very mixed - outstanding intellectuals, members of the elites, political party leaders, simple workers. Intellectually, they were more uniform - there was a custom among political prisoners to share knowledge and to educate fellow prisoners who had no formal education. They were social democrats, communists, catholics. However, one thing they had in common was that they all had rejected fascism and this imprisonment was their punishment. That group had learned hard lessons in the camp, and they operated by the motto, "We can be bent, but never broken". They were both very hard and very humane people.

Georg met me at the door to the Block and guided me to his table in the dining area of the barracks. There was a dish on the table, full of soup, a spoon and a piece of bread. The room was empty, everyone had moved outside to enjoy the warm sun. Georg said, "Please, be my guest and eat." Amazed, I sat down and began to eat the soup. He sat and struck up a conversation with me. While eating, I was also looking around the barracks. It was essentially the same as the block in which I lived. However, this room was very different. Our dining area was gloomy and the floor was covered by some kind of black pitch. The tables and benches were made of unpainted wood and had gone grey with age. The walls were also grey, unfinished wood. This space was very different. It was warm and friendly, the floor was painted a light colour, as were the walls. The tables and benches had the appearance of freshly polished wood. It was the same concentration camp, but it wasn't. When the dish was empty, I moved to wash it, but Georg would not let me. I was his guest.

For the next two weeks, Georg fed me. By then, I had recovered my health and no longer needed the supplementary food. Georg became my best, most trusted friend in the camp. We would meet in the evenings to talk about the future and about the world. We shared a dislike of Schopenhauer, and disagreed on the role of leading figures in history, but our visions of the future were similar in principle, albeit different in practical details - no wars, no terror, few prisons, no hunger, good health care, good social services, education accessible to everyone and friendly, happy people.

The other prisoners working in the office came from a variety of backgrounds. The financial division was populated mostly with German and Czech political prisoners, one of whom was the former Head of the National Library in Munich. One exception was Hans Geist, who was a Bevauer or BV - a criminal prisoner. He was not truly a criminal, but a wealthy man whose company had attracted the attention of someone powerful, for which he paid the consequences. He was a huge man, the only prisoner I knew of in the camp who was authorized to receive double portions of all meals. The technical division consisted mostly of Poles - myself as the chief designer, two technicians, three draftsmen and the two surveyors. There were also two Dutchmen (one, over sixty years old, a member of a very prestigious Amsterdam family and the other, a young man from Indonesia) and one Ukrainian, named Misha. All of us were political prisoners with the exception of a German, Erich, who wore the black triangular badge of an Asozial - "asocial prisoner". Erich was working in the Baubüro because of his talents. He was an exceptional precision draftsman able to imitate any design, currency or document. He was also a talented safecracker and I learned a lot from him about his former profession.

We were a select group and valuable property in the eyes of the SS. It was very dangerous for anyone, SS or prisoner, to hurt or kill someone who worked in the Baubüro and retaliation would be swift and deadly. So we enjoyed a special privileged position in the camp. As well, having easy access to writing materials and an ease of movement around and outside the camp meant that we also could accumulate the means to barter for various items stored in the Kanada, such as underwear, shoes, et cetera. We were entitled to leather shoes, clean clothes, a clean shirt. I was permitted to change my shirt twice a week and I had socks. It was also required that I wash my hands. And the food improved considerably, although there was still never enough. As Prominenten, we also could easily 'arrange' medical care if we fell ill, including medications. Even the SS officers of the camp thought twice before they struck a Prominent. For me, it was an enormous leap in status. I had been assigned to the post of chief designer. I had moved, overnight, from being one of the lowest in the camp, just above the Jews and Gypsies and one who could be easily killed by anyone in a position of authority, to the elevated status of Prominent who was carefully protected by strict written and unwritten rules.

Perhaps the most tangible manifestation of his change in status was the way in which Pindera moved between barracks. He moved in April 1942 from Block 16 to Block 46, an improvement according to his recollections. Still, it got quite crowded as the camp's prisoner intake climbed. At one point, the barracks were so crowded that the prisoners were sleeping three to a bunk. Pindera approached his Blockältester and requested permission to construct a bunk of his own. It was like a shelf built above the door to the dormitory. He argued that, as an engineer for the Baubüro, he needed to get a good night's sleep and could not do so when in a bunk with two others. Permission was granted. By 18 April 1943, Pindera had moved to a block for the Prominent, No. 6. And in July 1943, he moved into the block where he had initially taken the engineering exam and where Georg Saur lived, No. 4. Each physical shift marked his rise through the hierarchy of the prisoner community and his growing importance as a Prominent. The contrast between the circumstances of his first years in the camp, which very nearly killed him, and his life as a Prominent could not have been more marked. Not only had the move to the Baubüro literally saved his life, but it gave him opportunities and security that he never believed possible.

Because of the nature of the Baubüro's work, which included the inspection and supervision of construction sites, the prisoners who worked there were often outside of the camps. They were never without guards, but it did give them greater freedom. Pindera often went out of the camp with Staszek Wldolowski, a good friend and colleague from the Baubüro. Staszek was a surveyor and his work was very flexible. He would arrange his tasks so that he could do his outside work when the weather was fine. Pindera would often accompany him when he could create a pretext for doing so. Staszek would work very quickly, but accurately, and then to the dismay of their Ukrainian assistants who were carrying the survey instruments, he would find a well-protected piece of forest, lie down and sunbathe. Pindera would join him and the Ukrainians would keep watch, appearing to be very busy. It was a blissful few minutes.

Of course, even as Prominenten, they were constantly preoccupied with the search for food. Although Pindera reports that, as Prominenten, they were not starving, they were still always hungry. Because of their relative mobility and security, they had extraordinary opportunities to 'organize' food, and they could be very creative in its pursuit. For example, in the fall of 1944, Staszek came up with an idea....

Staszek decided it was important to inspect the bakery. He was concerned that the structure might not be sound, and he wanted to check it for deformations resulting from 'age-induced deterioration.' I, of course, was concerned that the main supporting beams could carry the load of new equipment that had been installed. So we were permitted to visit the bakery, although we went separately to avoid raising suspicions. The foreman at the bakery knew instantly why we were really there, and so he prepared several two-kilogramme loaves of delicious, dark bread for each of us. We cut the loaves lengthwise, so we could fit them under our clothes. Staszek left first and made it safely to the Baubüro, where he distributed the bread among our fellow prisoners, as was the custom. Then it was my turn. I was wearing the usual thin uniform, but also had a relatively new jacket from Kanada. The jacket was a thick one, which helped disguise my added padding, but it didn't hide it completely. This didn't seem insurmountable. My guard was a young soldier who would never have dreamed that a prisoner would be so bold nor did he know me well, so he didn't notice the change in my appearance.

Everything was going well as I returned to the camp, until I met Bauleiter Schnöll, who ran the Baubüro. I was required to salute him in the usual way of the camp, and wait for him to dismiss me. But rather than dismissing me with the usual 'Carry on," he looked at me oddly and asked me how I had become so thick. My heart stopped. I looked him in the eye, and told him that, as the weather was a bit fresh, I had dressed warmly. He nodded and told me to carry on. A few minutes later, I too was in the Baubüro, where I reported to Richard that I had returned and then distributed the bread among my fellow prisoners in the office, reserving a double portion of the bread for myself - the customary fee of the 'organizer'.

Pindera and Staszek pulled a similar caper at the meatpacking shop. On one visit there, the shop was stuffing sausages, and they managed to 'organize' some of them. They couldn't take the large sausages, because they were too hard to hide, but they could easily hide links of small sausages. They strung them across their shoulders and down their sleeves. They tied them around their waists. They hung them down their pant legs. Of course, they realized after they had left the meatpackers that they had to be careful, because they could not salute. If they raised their arm to salute, the sausages would stick out their sleeves! But they managed to get back to the Baubüro without incident.

Another amusing incident happened only a few weeks after the visit to the bakery. Staszek and I decided to check the possibility of organizing food from Major Skorzeny's headquarters. He was the commander of a special unit of SS, a SWAT team of sorts. One of his most famous exploits was rescuing Benito Mussolini from house arrest. Skorzeny had commissioned the Baubüro to build a riding arena and I was the designer assigned to the project. The official purpose of the visit was to inspect the properties of the soil at the site, so we could determine what the arena needed by way of a foundation. Staszek had to survey the site before we could draft blueprints. However, we also knew there would be good food at Skorzeny's headquarters, because this was a very special unit. We just didn't know how to get at it. So I grabbed a bundle of blueprints that could serve as camouflage, and we walked to the site, several kilometres away. We would figure it out when we got there.

We met Skorzeny himself when we got there. I needed to speak to him about what he wanted in the arena and we had to report in. Skorzeny answered our questions, and then gave us permission to move around the site as needed. Meanwhile, our escort had stopped off at the guardroom for the headquarters. I had noticed a wide channel of flowing water close by, as we had walked into the camp, and so I got bold and asked Skorzeny if I could go for a swim. As a youth, I had enjoyed swimming greatly and had not been able to swim since I had been captured in early 1940. It was an audicious request, but he smiled and told me that I could! He assigned one of his own soldiers as my guard, and to my surprise and delight, the soldier did not carry a weapon. At the channel's side, I realized I did not have swimming trunks. The soldier also noticed my dilemma, and unbelievably, he turned his back to me while I stripped, only turning back again when he heard that I was in the water. I enjoyed that swim tremendously. It was small pleasures like this, a swim or a chance to soak up sunshine for a few minutes, that helped make our internment bearable.

Having returned from the swim, I checked the construction site with Staszek. Everything appeared fine. The soil was good and the foundations would not require any special handling. Access to the site was straightforward. Everything seemed in order for the project, so we could turn our attention to the real purpose of our trip, organizing food.

It looked promising, but first we had to get some kind of container for the food. Staszek knew the foreman at the headquarters, so he gave us a chest with a lid. We did not dare organize meat, fat or cheese, so we filled the chest with potatoes, rye, flour and vegetables. We loaded the chest into a wheelbarrow to transport it. I had the blueprints to spread out on top of the wheelbarrow to hide the chest.

We had two inspection points to pass through, one when leaving Skorzeny's compound and one when we entered Sachsenhausen. It was a significant risk, but one we were willing to take. In fact, we were not inspected when we left the compound, which was a relief. However, the wheelbarrow was heavy and the distance back to Sachsenhausen was several kilometres. At one point, the wheelbarrow landed in a ditch. Fortunately, the lid of the chest didn't spring open - that would have been a disaster. But Staszek and I were not strong enough to get the wheelbarrow back on the road. As we struggled with it, suddenly the SS guard who was escorting us put his gun on his back and helped us lift the wheelbarrow out of the ditch. We couldn't believe it, the SS helping us to 'organize' food. We also cleared the gate at Sachsenhausen without incident. We immediately took the food to a friend of mine, Paul. Paul worked in a small shack where he melted down scrap metal to be sent on to a metalworking factory. This meant he had a source of heat and pots. He was an old prisoner [*meaning he had been in the camp for a very long time*], so he knew how to cooperate. He took our supplies and made soup for all the prisoners of the Baubüro, as well as himself. Each man received about two litres of very thick, nourishing soup. It was a small thing, but important at that time.

Sometimes there were occasions to relax completely. One such occasion was when our Czech colleagues in the office came up with a crazy idea - to give a concert in the Baubüro during the Easter holidays. As in many concentration camps, we had a prisoners' orchestra, so musical instruments were available. Other instruments were requisitioned from Kanada. Richard very indirectly approached the Bauleiter, who quickly understood what was being implied and announced that he would be absent from the Baubüro that day. The Bauführers got an inkling of what was being planned and generally made it clear that they preferred not to be interested. The Czechs smuggled in the instruments, as well as a talented Czech musician. And three young Bauführers asked if they could attend! We happily agreed to their request - if nothing else, it gave us some protection. The concert, as I remember it, was marvellous. It started with Dvorak, in honour of the Czechs who organized it, but there was also Bach, Mozart, Chopin and Beethoven. I particularly remember the Beethoven, because it was the first time in my life that I understood him.

In fact, there were a considerable number and variety of cultural activities built into daily life in the camp. These cultural activities, as Pindera suggested, maintained and strengthen the prisoners' morale and overcame their sense of isolation. There were cabarets, plays, concerts. Instruments were smuggled into the camp and there was a complete string quartet made up of prisoners who performed regularly, led by a Czech virtuoso violinist (perhaps the same Czech who performed in the Baubüro that Sunday afternoon). This little orchestra practised clandestinely in the delousing station, where it was reasonably safe to believe the SS would not stumble upon them. The SS did not like entering the building for fear of becoming infested. In the midst of a scarlet fever epidemic, a choir was formed. As one prisoner recalled, as hundreds died daily, the choir continued to sing. Even as they froze, starved and died, this man explained, at least in the evenings they had music and song. The prisoner administration established a library in the camp, with an amazingly wide variety of works available. Once a prisoner had been in the camp for a year, he was given access to the library and allowed to borrow up to one book a month. Pindera himself took great advantage of the library - that is where he was first introduced to Schopenhauer, for example. He learned German by reading the Nazi newspaper, the "Volkischer Beobachter". He also developed his German vocabulary by memorizing ten words a day. He did this by copying out the day's words on a scrap of paper, tucking it in his hat, and pulling it out whenever he had a moment during the day. Of course, if he had been caught practising his German in such a way during the workday, he would have faced, at best, severe punishment. Nonetheless, he soon was functioning in the language, which was a decided advantage, as he could then understand the commands of the SS, as well as write his own letters to his mother.

Initially, the cultural activities were strictly prohibited and secrecy was crucial. However, by 1942 and 1943, the SS administration was much more tolerant and these activities gained a semi-legal status. This may have been a reflection of their half-hearted efforts to increase prisoner productivity. Apparently, the restrictions lessened so much that prisoners even sold tickets to other prisoners for some of the concerts and shows. Songs and singing were life's blood for the prisoners, helping them get through the long days and cold nights. Sunday concerts became a standing event. They became known as "Sachsenhausen wie noch nie - Sachsenhausen as it never was." They were a sort of theatre of the nations. Prisoners from each nation were given a short time on stage to present vignettes of their country's culture and life. The performances could get rather elaborate, according to Pindera. Costumes were made in the KZ shops. The Polish group once performed the national dance, the krakowiak. Another time, a good friend of Pindera's, Janusz Wellenger, danced as a girl in proper folk costume against a backdrop of the old Polish castle of Wawel in Krakow. The French prisoners sang French songs. And then the event would end with a gesture of international solidarity. These gradually became too politicized for the liking of the SS and, after one rather spectacular performance, future such events were banned. The oldest German prisoner in the camp had come on the stage, apologized for having to speak in German, and called for a demonstration of national solidarity by saying, "We Germans, we call upon you." He was then joined on stage by representatives of each of the twenty-three nations found in Sachsenhausen, one by one in alphabetical order. Each came on the stage and announced their presence, "We Belgians! We French! We Polish! We Yugoslavs!", and so on. When all the nations were on the stage, everyone, audience and performers, chanted, "We join you. Always together, never alone." The purpose of these gestures was simple, to bolster the morale of the prisoners and bind them closer together. In this way the SS could be defeated, Pindera argued, because one of the objectives of the SS was to break the prisoners' spirits. If one could combat the terror that the SS tried to instil, that was an important part of the battle. The cultural events helped to do that. These moments of relaxation and 'beating the system' were precious, for they not only nourished the body, they also nourished the spirit and soul.

Another source of sustenance, physical as well as spiritual and moral, was the constant correspondence with his mother and sister, as well as the steady stream of money and packages they sent to him. By August 1942, the instructions on the forms used by the prisoners to write to the outside world had changed. Previously, packages were strictly forbidden, although, as we have seen, Pindera's mother seemed to have circumvented that restriction. Then a typewritten notice was attached to the letter Pindera wrote to his mother on 23 August 1942. It said that prisoners would be allowed sweaters, shirts, underwear, socks, handkerchiefs and gloves. The following remained specifically forbidden: food, photos, letters or other inclosures. His mother and other friends began sending him socks, sweaters, winter underwear and money. And while food was apparently forbidden, a regular supply of provisions still made its way to Pindera, ranging from zweiback and bread to fruit, potted chicken and duck, and chocolate. The packages seem to arrive regularly, every two weeks or so. In addition, he continued to receive money orders of 10, 20 and even 50 Reichmarks on a regular basis. By the summer of 1944, he was almost embarrassed by his mother's largesse, as well as concerned that she might be suffering herself, in order to provide him with food and clothing. In July 1944, he wrote his mother telling her that he needed nothing more and she should stop sending parcels and money orders, that he thought she needed it more than him - a revealing comment. His concern for his mother's well-being was clear, but it also suggestive of his improved circumstances. It is interesting that all of these goods made it to him without pilferage. One would have expected it to have disappeared long before it reached Pindera. But the staff in the camp's post office were Jehovah's Witnesses and resolutely honest. Nothing was stolen from the mail once it was in their hands.

Meanwhile, the work continued....

The design projects we were normally assigned were not for sensitive or secret structures. As we were almost all political prisoners, accused of high treason, we could not be trusted with such projects.

This suited us, because it was quite dangerous to one's health to be involved in such things. Generally, those who worked on these kinds of structures died soon after completion, taking the secrets with them. Only once was a top secret project sent to the Baubüro. It was to design a device that would transport German agents to North America. Richard had told the Bauleiter that none of the Germans in the office could work on it, because their sentences of high treason made them ineligible. Unfortunately my sentence was only a death sentence, so I was eligible. It was a project dreamed up by a German prisoner, a former SS officer who had been imprisoned for something like either corruption or homosexual activity and who was trying to save himself by being ingratiating. He came up with the idea of using the Heinkel 177 airplane to transport agents to North America. It had a reach of 6000 kilometres and flew at enormous heights, up to 8000 or 9000 metres. This was far too high for an agent to jump from the plane. So he devised a means for the agent to jump in two stages. First the agent would jump in a container and when he had reached a safe height, he would get out of the container, open a second parachute and then continue to the ground. The Baubüro was given the task to design this device. I was frightened. Thankfully, Richard was able to persuade Schnöll to get me released from the project. I returned to the Baubüro after two days, a very happy man. A few months later, I heard that the head of that design group had been executed.

Even before I was in the Baubüro, I was almost trapped in a similar way. Dr. von Braun, a noted German scientist, was starting to experiment with ballistic rockets and he needed people to calculate trajectories and orbits. This, remember, was long before calculators, let alone computers. Somebody came to my block, looking for prisoners who knew mathematics. I was recruited, but once I started working on the project, I got scared. I knew what this was all about, I had taken a course on rocket propulsion in school and so the phrase set off alarm bells in my head. As soon as I could, I excused myself from the team, arguing my attention span was not good enough and that my knowledge of mathematics was very poor. Staying on that Kommando would have put me in the same situation as the Jewish specialists who were forging foreign currencies in Falschwerkstatt - marvellous living conditions, great food and assured death at the end of the war. (*The purpose of the Falschwerkstatt was to disrupt the enemy economies by flooding them with paper currency. This Kommando also forged foreign stamps and identity papers.*) Nor could I work directly against the Allies, as I considered myself still a soldier and officer of the Polish Army and at war with the Germans, although I didn't say that to them, of course. Thankfully, my excuses were accepted and I left that team, as well.

Otherwise, I was involved in a variety of construction projects. In one case, as mentioned earlier, I was ordered to design a riding arena for Major Skorzeny and his forces. Skorzeny put a great of emphasis on the physical training of his troops and he had decided that his men needed to learn how to ride a horse. To do this, he needed an indoor arena for training, as winter in northern Germany is nasty. His headquarters were in a castle about 10 or 15 kilometres from Sachsenhausen and so the Baubüro was given the job of designing it. The design of that structure gave me a lot of satisfaction. It was an interesting exercise in building wide spans because it could not have any pillars in the middle of the arena, but had to be 26 metres across and at least 40 metres long. Since I had a free hand in its design, I chose to build a timber frame structure with connectors made of high-strength, alloy steel. It was, in the end, a beautiful structure and one of which I was very proud.

Another building with which I was involved did not inspire the same kind of feelings. It was called Herz As, or Heart's Ace. It was a magnificent, but repulsive structure. I had not designed it, but I supervised its construction. The building accomodated a wireless installation for communication with German personnel everywhere in the world and its design reflected its strategic importance. It was made of reinforced concrete with three-dimensional reinforcement, using reinforcing rods two centimetres thick and spaced twenty centimetres apart. Because of this, we had to use a special kind of fluid concrete and it had to be cast continuously, day and night. The structure left an impression of brutal might. The steeply raked roof was five and a half meters thick; the walls were four metres thick; the floor plate, four and a half metres; and the inside walls, three metres thick. The whole building was placed in a young forest, so carefully camouflaged.

Another project left me with mixed feelings. It came late in the war. The Warsaw Uprising in the summer of 1944 had taught the Germans a valuable lesson - that a city's sewers could be used effectively in a military conflict, as a means of moving about and transporting goods and people. A few months after that disastrous rebellion, I was ordered to redesign the outlets of the camp's sewage system. All the outlets were to be replaced with new, very narrow reinforced concrete outlets. I did it, but with much reluctance - once again I was producing an installation that had the clear purpose of confining or destroying me.

Nonetheless, Pindera generally found the design process, as well as the supervision of construction, a rewarding experience, one in which he took pride and often joy. He thrived on the intellectual challenge and on the sheer fact that he was learning, once again, as well as getting to practice his chosen profession. When Pindera wrote his mother in February 1942 to tell her of his good fortune to be transferred to the Baubüro, the excitement was tangible...

> Nevertheless I thank you for the news of my brother - because of his last job I send him heartfelt wishes with the hope that his Chief is completely pleased with his technical knowledge. I wait also with impatience for all the news from him, and wish him luck in his construction work! ...
> (22 February 1942)

His enthusiasm for the job remained unabated, that was clear when he wrote his mother...

> Thank you for the news about Tadek; it pleases me that he has now such responsible and independent work - I believe that he now has no desire to find another position. (14 June 1942)

And even into 1943, Pindera was still wondering at the sheer joy he derived from the intellectual challenge and growth, as he explained to his mother...

> Here all is in order, I am feeling relatively content, in free time, I read a lot, I have learned a lot - I never expected that the work could give such contentment, such happiness; so much so that if I could see and speak to you, then I would lack nothing more!" (27 June 1943)

and

> I am learning much work, therefore the time passes quickly for me. Now I can honestly say - the years here have not

been a complete loss - quite the opposite - I have learned
my work, and I like to work! This is important!
(11 July 1943)

*It was the intellectual challenge and the opportunity to continue to
learn that resonated with Pindera, as well as the relative security that
came with being a Prominent and safe within the walls of the Baubüro.
There was also a sense of freedom that came with the job - being able
to leave the camp, if only temporarily, in order to inspect a
construction site; to be able to climb to the top of the scaffolding of a
structure and be above the camp or the site, alone; to be able to lose
himself in the details of a project; and through the design process, let
his mind stretch beyond the barbed wire that confined his physical
body. He had to be careful to not let this lull him into a false sense of
security however, as his tentative freedom and independence, his very
life, could be easily and brutally snatched from him, and at any
moment. It would only take one small slip.*

*Nonetheless, he became quite bold. In a letter to his mother dated
21 March 1943, he asked her to send him a textbook by Professor
Timoshenko, entitled "Festigkeitslehre". Pindera had had the request
cleared by Schnöll, arguing that he needed the book for his work. It
took a while for his mother to find the book, as he wrote on 11 July that
she could find the book at the Technical Bookstore in Warsaw, if
nowhere else. She finally tracked it down and sent it, and then all hell
broke loose. When the book arrived, it had to be cleared through the
Central Office. One bright-eyed SS officer noticed the author's name,
and alarms went off. This is because the Battle of Kursk had just
happened, in which the German armies had been soundly defeated by
the Russian forces, who had been led by a General Timoshenko. An SS
officer was dispatched to the Baubüro, who hauled Pindera into the
office of the Rapportführer to explain why he was in contact with
General Timoshenko! It was a tough fifteen minutes until he could
convince the Rapportführer that there were two different Timoshenkos.
What saved Pindera was that the two had different first names.*

*It was not just the intellectual challenge, however, that gave
Pindera purpose. Working in the Baubüro provided him with an
opportunity to strike back at the Germans. He could do that by
exploiting his role as a designer to create structures that excessively
consumed resources necessary to the Reich's war effort. Ironically,
Pindera was simply putting Nazi principles into action. The Reich was*

*intended to last one thousand years, and there was a strong emphasis
on beauty in strength and in the architecture of the regime. So Pindera
decided that he would design structures that would last one thousand
years and would be as beautiful as he could make them, no matter the
cost or how pedestrian the structure's purpose. Or rather, he designed
them with an eye to maximizing the cost. This meant that not only
would the buildings be strong, but they would be made with the most
expensive and rarest materials he could obtain. If he could persuade
his immediate supervisors of the necessity of using these materials,
then no one would question it, because no one dared question the SS,
not even about the materials it might requisition for its projects.
Second, he could strike back by working to protect fellow prisoners
from the savagery of the camp system, as much as he could, given his
job as construction supervisor and designer. It was a tightrope he
chose to walk, but it was a tangible and effective way he could continue
a war he had never really abandoned. His position as designer gave
him some protection and also some power, which he used willingly.
For instance, Pindera had heard from fellow prisoners that the SS-
Bauführer who supervised the Kommando SS Kino regularly beat the
prisoners at this site. That Kommando was working on one of the
construction sites for which Pindera was responsible. He timed his
arrival on the site for a moment when he knew the Bauführer would be
there.*

I learned that on one of the construction sites that I had designed,
one of the SS Bauführers was still beating the prisoners. It was not
allowed, a law had been passed banning such beatings. (*This was
Himmler's decree of December 1942.*) But he was still doing it. So I
went there for an inspection. I ensured that I would arrive when he
would be there. I told him that I would like to inspect the site under the
order of Schnöll, and that it would be better if we walked through the
site together. We went to the second floor, where the prisoners were
laying brick. We were walking along the scaffolding, when that
Bauführer, who was apparently unhappy with something that one of the
prisoners had done, kicked the prisoner in the face. He almost knocked
him off the scaffolding. I got angry, very angry, but this was my
opportunity. I raised my voice slightly, taking care that I did not overdo
it, and said, "Now I know why the walls are deficient – the prisoners
are afraid. The Bauleiter always says that we are in the third year of
war and must make every effort to make our work efficient. Prisoners

who are kicked do not work efficiently. I am obliged to report this event to the Bauleiter." I really used the words *"Wir sind in dritten Kriegsjahr"* – "we are in the third year of the war". Me, a political prisoner, reminding an SS officer that Germany was still at war! And I told him that if he did it again, I would be obliged to report it to the Bauleiter. I heard later that he never beat a prisoner again. He would have been sent to the East Front if he had. It was a small thing, but for the prisoners, especially in 1944, to die in such a stupid way.... That would have been a travesty.

So Pindera could make a difference. However, he was not invulnerable...

I had some problems when designing the automotive depot, a repair shop for vehicles. It was a large building, about forty metres wide, sixty metres long and twelve metres high. The shop was for repairing various types of military vehicles coming from the Eastern Front and so it was a quite large structure. Because of the design conditions, my structural solution had to be based on continuous three-span reinforced beams, of a total length of forty metres. The lower beam was supported by four columns made of high strength, hard bricks. When the lower beam was cast, four brick columns were erected and the second reinforced beam was cast. The lower beam carried a light concrete wall. There were problems with the design code, however, because its formula for calculating the stress in such a structure was incorrect and it neglected to take into account the interaction between the wall and the supporting beam. I had to guess at the load distribution on the lower beam. As a result, in the blueprints, I had directed that the scaffold supporting the cast beam be left in place for four weeks, to ensure that it had cured and set properly. The foreman of the automotive depot's Kommando was a criminal prisoner who did not like it when I suggested that the members of his Kommando not be treated harshly and, perhaps, did not like the "gentlemen" from the Baubüro. Thus, he found a pretext to violate my directions and removed the scaffold supporting the lower beam before the four weeks were over. The result was easy to foresee – the lower beam developed cracks. This should have been fatal for me and the Kommando, given the rules of life in the KZ. Fortunately, the SS badly needed that building because of the losses at the Eastern Front and they could not afford to destroy its builders. Thankfully, I had put my directions in writing on the blueprints and so could prove to the

Bauleiter that the damage was the fault of the Bauführer. Schnöll simply told me to find a remedy, which I did.

There were other instances when projects went awry and the results should have been the death of both Pindera and the other prisoners involved. Often Pindera was able to salvage the situation and prevent punishment. Once, he had designed a reinforced concrete ramp. He decided to visit the site, just as they were pouring the concrete. When he arrived, they had just started and he discovered, to his dismay, that the foreman on the site had installed the reinforcing rods incorrectly. The finished ramp would have collapsed under any kind of load, almost immediately. This was a very dangerous situation for all. So he ordered the Kommando to dig a huge and deep hole behind the building, cut out and break up the concrete that had been poured and bury the offending ramp. They then built a new one, this time, properly reinforced.

Several times, Pindera almost went too far in challenging the SS authorities, but one time in particular, he was certain that he was going to die for his audacity. He had openly refused to carry out an express order from Schnöll. It all began when Schnöll called Pindera into his office....

It was first thing in the morning. The bell on Richard's desk rang just as we were entering the main office. It was Schnöll summoning Richard to his office. After a while, Richard returned and told me that Schnöll wanted to see me. This was unusual, but when I asked Richard the reason, he was non-committal. That meant the matter had to be serious. I knocked on the door and heard, "Come in." As was the protocol, I announced, "Prisoner 28 862 requests permission to enter." Having been told to enter, I approached the desk of the Bauleiter and stood at attention, as required. The Bauleiter asked whether I remembered designing the roof for the SS Theater. I remembered it very well because I was very proud of that structure. I designed the roof as a system of girders like airplane wings, very light. The girders were made of the highest quality of pine using the newly developed technology of timber structures with special connectors and high strength nails, as was required by the newest design code. It was a very expensive design, consuming costly materials, but it was elegant. So I answered affirmatively, that indeed I remembered it. Schnöll directed me to go to the construction site, inspect the situation there and return with a report about the state of the site. It was clear what kind of a report he expected me to submit - he used the word *Schweinerei*, meaning that it looked like a pigsty, to describe the situation there. He asked me whether I understood his order and I replied that I did. I left his office and told Richard about the order I had received. Richard made no comments nor any suggestions, which was a very bad sign. Then I collected the blueprints for the theatre from my desk, went to the guardroom and asked for a guard to accompany me to the site.

You see, site inspections were a regular part of the Baubüro's business. Yet, naturally, prisoners could not be allowed outside of the camp on their own or even from one part of the camp to another. So an escort system had been devised. A prisoner authorized to leave the Baubüro went to the guardroom and requested a guard. They then registered his destination at the gate and the prisoner and guard walked to the destination. Normally, for me, it gave me a certain feeling of freedom, for the guard normally walked behind me. If I stretched my imagination, I could almost ignore the loaded gun at my back. This trip, however, I was too preoccupied to think about feelings of freedom. It was thirty minutes to the theatre and I had to do some serious planning.

I knew the SS officer who was the Bauführer of the SS Theater. Prisoners did not have any civil rights and were not allowed to sign business documents, thus although the work on the construction site was actually directed and supervised by a foreman, who was a prisoner, each site had a Bauführer who could sign the documents and who was formally responsible for the progress of the work. This particular Bauführer was unusual. He had a degree that was the equivalent of a North American Masters degree in Engineering, but his SS rank was the lowest possible. He was very tolerant, very polite and never objected to the use of the Polish language. If I were to do as ordered and report gross inefficiency at the site, this Bauführer would be sent to the Eastern Front and almost certain death and at least some of the prisoners on the site would certainly be killed, slowly and painfully, charged with sabotage. I decided that I could not be a part of such an act. The implications of that choice, however, were sobering and my heart sank.

I arrived at the construction site, where the SS guard joined the other guards. I inspected the site. Indeed, it was messy and some expensive construction materials had been wasted. I then went to the foreman's shack and informed him that the Bauleiter had ordered me to inspect the site and report to him all the *Schweinerei* that I noticed. The

foreman was an old political prisoner and understood the situation.
"What will you report?" he asked me. "It depends on you," I replied,
"How many people do you have?" "Sixty," was his answer. I looked
around again, and checked the time - it was nine a.m. I made a fast
calculation in my head and said to him, "You have five hours to restore
order. Forget the noon meal break. And no walking, only running!"
That was all I could do to help and the foreman understood that. He left
without a word. I stayed in the shack. I could hear him raise his voice
outside, as he ordered the prisoners to work. I looked through the
window and saw a half-sleepy construction site transformed into a busy
beehive of activity. The noon hour came and passed, without a break.
This was backbreaking work and the prisoners certainly hated me for it.
They could not understand or be told the reason for the haste, and
probably believed it was just a matter of a Prominent asserting his
power. They certainly did not realize that this was saving their lives and
the foreman could not tell them that or his head would roll. It was soon
clear that the site would be back in order by three p.m., which is when I
planned to return to the office. The prisoners and the foreman would be
safe. However, I was not.

By doing what I had done, I had openly refused to follow an order
explicitly given to me by the Bauleiter, who wanted a report from me
about the atrocious conditions on the site. This was blatant
insubordination and it had to be punished severely and publicly. My
chances of surviving were nil. I wracked my brain for a solution. I did
not want to die, but I saw no way out that was honourable. I had to
refuse to carry out the order, even if it meant death. My only hope lay
with the Bauleiter himself, and with the fact that only three people
knew about the nature of the order - the Bauleiter, Richard and myself.
If I could persuade the Bauleiter that my solution to the problem on the
site solved his objection and no one else knew about the order, he just
might be persuaded to spare me. He was certainly a decent man. He
allowed us to speak Polish in the office and he even forgave small
breaches of discipline. He had introduced a very humane atmosphere
into the Baubüro. Nonetheless, I had directly disobeyed his order and
the punishment for such a crime was typically twenty-five to fifty
lashes, followed by hanging. I did not have much hope.

At three p.m., I returned to the office and reported to Richard.
Richard told me to wait, and told the Bauleiter I was there. A few
minutes later, I was summoned into the Bauleiter's office. I gathered
my courage and knocked on his door. Hearing "Enter", I entered his

office and my heart sank. While I was supervising the restoration of the construction site, Schnöll had summoned to his office all the Bauführers - about thirty SS officers. So the matter was no longer just between him and me - it was now very public. It was a disaster. I knew I could not change my decision - I could not live with the dishonour. But I also knew this would force Schnöll's hand - he could not ignore my gross insubordination, otherwise he himself would be punished harshly. So it was the end. There was no hope for me. A thought crossed my mind - I had been negligent. On the way back to the Baubüro, I should have stopped at the hospital for a cyanide pill, just in case. Now, it was too late.

I took a deep breath and began the ritualistic formula, "Prisoner 28 862 requests...", but Schnöll interrupted me and said graciously, "No, Pindera, report on the chaos that you have just seen." His voice was relaxed, but the atmosphere in the room was very tense. My reply was what I had prepared in advance, "Yes, Obersturmführer, I carefully inspected the site. I noticed numerous small deficiencies typical for a construction site of that type; the deficiencies were corrected and at this time the construction site is in the best order." I waited. There was not a sound in the office, the silence was complete. The Bauleiter looked at me in disbelief and his face became redder and redder. He shouted, "*RAUS!*" and I began to stammer out the formula a prisoner recites before leaving the presence of an SS officer. He cut me off with another furious "*Raus!*", and I quickly left the room and returned to my desk.

That whole office was silent, shocked. They had heard it all. I sat at my desk in a stupor. After fifteen minutes, the door between the main office and the Bauleiter's office opened. All the Bauführers walked out, and passed my desk on their way out. They were very somber. The Bauführer from the SS Theater gave me a sad half-smile, which I returned. Nothing could save me. The Bauleiter had to report my insubordination, as too many people knew about it, or he would be accused of gross negligence. At best, he would be stripped of his rank and sent to the Eastern Front. Simply put, he could not afford to try to save me.

The silence deepened in our office. Suddenly the bell on Richard's desk rang. In the silence, it sounded shrill. Richard got up, entered the Bauleiter's office, and then returned, quietly approaching my desk. "Jerzy, go to the Chief." I stood up and entered the Bauleiter's office, reciting the required formula. We were alone. The Obersturmführer was sitting at his desk, with both hands on top of it, staring at me. "How dare you disobey my order?!" The words were harsh, but amazingly, the tone was not. Rather, it was the tone of a concerned man. That was encouraging, so I decided to tell him the truth. I replied, "Any other report would not be compatible with my technical conscience." He was intrigued, if not puzzled, and he asked me to explain. And so I did, forgetting that I was talking to my deadly enemy. It was a conversation between professionals and intellectuals, about ethical standards.

The conversation lasted about one hour. In the end, the Bauleiter indicated that he understood my position and did not oppose my decision. There was a silence of several minutes, while he thought. Then he told me that, from then on, I would regularly carry out systematic inspections of all construction sites I designed. The implication was that I was now responsible for the state of all sites for which I did the design. Then he dismissed me, almost giving me the Nazi salute as I left, but just catching himself in time. I gave the appropriate formulaic phrases and left the room, stunned. I was not going to die! Instead, I had been given more authority! Richard, anxious, asked if everything was okay. I said it was and everyone, bewildered, relaxed. I was and have always been awed by Schnöll's choice. He chose to risk his rank, his position, his life and his family's well-being because he understood and agreed with my decision and reasons for it.

Pindera's resistance activities did not just entail trying to save fellow prisoners from punishment and death, although that was an important part of it. He was also determined to steal from the Nazi war effort as much as possible, by using his design projects to siphon off resources needed for the war machine. As mentioned, one example of those efforts was the construction of the SS Theater, in which he used top grade wood and steel. He also used the most expensive concrete for his structures and the most expensive steel for reinforcing it. He actually once tried stainless steel for reinforcing concrete but it was a disaster, as the concrete would not grip the steel. When he ordered wood, it was airplane quality - strong, smooth, without knots... and expensive. He had to be careful, because if someone watched too closely they would see what he was doing. In fact, at one point, he was challenged for this very thing. He was designing a Ballonhalle, or building for manufacturing balloons, at the time.

I suggested a timber structure for the Ballonhalle and the idea was accepted. Of course, I chose to build it using a high quality, aircraft grade of pine and to apply the newest technology of the moment - stainless steel connectors and high strength nails. I based the design on the newly published design code and based my plans on the then-current designs for the wings of aircraft and sailplanes. This required high strength and low weight pine girders. The span was about 15 metres. I was very pleased with my design when I submitted the calculations and blueprints for approval by the Bauleiter.

A week later, I was summoned to the Bauleiter's office. He informed me that specialists from the Bauinspektion der Bauleitung, the Construction Inspection Office of the parent company, questioned my calculations and plans and recommended changes. Schnöll obviously wanted me to incorporate the recommendations, but I could not do so. If I let the changes be made without a fight, then there was a real possibility that all my future designs would be scrutinized closely and I would lose my means of resisting. I needed to have a free hand in my design and in the choice of materials. So I replied to Schnöll that I could not do so, as my design was assuredly correct.

A few days later, two SS officers from the Inspection Office appeared in the Baubüro to inspect my design more closely and to speak with me about it. We spread out my calculations and blueprints on Richard's desk. These officers were a different breed - obviously well-bred gentlemen. It was the rule in the Baubüro that prisoners had to remain standing when addressed by an SS officer from outside the office (we could remain sitting when dealing with an SS officer from within). Thus, I had to remain standing while the two officers were offered chairs. When they realized that I had remained standing, the two glanced at each other rapidly and decided to remain standing themselves. The same dance occurred when they wanted to smoke. Again, the prisoners were strictly forbidden to smoke during working hours, so I could not. At one point, one of the officers took out his cigarette case, but the other looked at him and then looked at me. The first then put the case back in his pocket, without comment. So the three of us stood around Richard's desk, discussing my design. I presented my design concept and explained the accuracy of my calculations. They listened without interruption and when I had finished, they asked a series of questions which I answered as well as I could. It appeared they were more concerned about the safety of the structure than the cost, although it would be an expensive building. The whole discussion lasted over three hours, but in the end, I had convinced them. The higher ranking officer looked at me, and said, "Thank you, it is all right." I got a green light and there was no further questioning of my designs.

The most dangerous game Pindera played during his internment was when he was reassigned to the Heinkel factory.

Not far from the main concentration camp of Sachsenhausen was a satellite camp in the village of Germensdorf. It held approximately seven thousand prisoners who were employed at the airplane factory Heinkel Flugzeug Werke. This was a modern airplane factory producing cutting-edge aircraft, both heavy bombers and lighter, smaller planes. I hoped that, with my background, I would be assigned to servicing the airplanes being used for testing or to the design office, which would have access to the airfield. If things worked out properly, I could perhaps even steal a plane and escape. At worst, with my knowledge of aeronautical engineering, I could inflict serious damage to the German air effort.

I spoke to Harry Naujoks, the Lagerältester, about my wish to transfer. He was a key figure in the communist leadership and the resistance in the camp and he was also responsible for assigning work details for the prisoners. He could arrange the transfer easily, if he approved of it. He spoke to Richard Adler and the two arranged my transfer. The tacit agreement was that I would continue my resistance efforts at Heinkel and if things went wrong there, I would be transferred back to the Baubüro. So in the fall of 1942, I was transferred to the satellite camp in Germensdorf.

When I was transferred, it was with a group of about twenty other prisoners. I was the only one interrogated; however, not by SS officers, but by men in civilian clothes - presumably management from the Heinkelwerke. They asked me my profession and I replied that I was an aeronautical engineer, with a specialization in the structure of airplanes. They then asked with which types of Polish planes I was familiar. I told them that I knew the Polish sport plane RWD-8, the light fighter PZL-24 and the brand new Polish bomber, the Los. When they asked what I was able to do, I replied that I could easily work in the design office or service test planes. This ended the questions and the men retreated to consult with themselves, while I continued to stand at attention, cap in hand. After fifteen minutes of discussion, I was informed that I would be assigned to the fuselage assembly line as a craftsman.

This was a catastrophe! There was no way I could possibly get access to a plane to escape if I was on the assembly line. My plans collapsed. It was clear to me that they had seen my file and knew my sentence. Worse still, I was assigned to the night shift, from six o'clock in the afternoon to six o'clock in the morning. Working the night shift meant that it was impossible to get more than four or five hours of sleep each day and that would be deadly in the long run. It was obvious that I had been thwarted and that I could do little at Heinkel. I decided to contact the resistance in the main camp and arrange for my return to the Baubüro. There would be no trouble getting a replacement for me, the assignment was an attractive one - there were no beatings, no killings. One worked under a roof and had warm, comfortable quarters in which to live, with hot showers available all the time. So I told my friends in Saschsenhausen about the situation and continued to work the night shift, using the opportunity to improve my French, Russian and Ukrainian while I awaited my transfer. The Kommando to which I was assigned was a polyglot of nationalities - Germans, Poles, French, Russians, Ukrainians, Yugoslavs. I was given the responsibilities of a foreman, but not the rights, which suited me fine. As few of these men understood German, my chief task was to translate the instructions of the supervising civilian technician for my fellow prisoners. The work was easy. We were responsible for rivetting together the shell of the fuselage.

Several days later, I received catastrophic news - the core of the resistance in Sachsenhausen had been arrested on 1 October, including Harry Naujoks. They had all been brutally tortured, but had survived it and were now dispersed to other concentration camps. It meant that, for all practical purposes, I was stranded on the moon - with no connections, no friends, no support, no lifeline. The resistance organisation in the main camp had been blown apart. And I was no longer a Prominent, as I had slid down the KZ hierarchy with my transfer and appointment as foreman at the Heinkelwerke. The only protection was that I was now considered an old prisoner. My number, 28 862, was a low one and that told others that I was tough, someone not to antagonize, because I had survived years in the camp. My 'age' afforded me some protection, then.

The collapse of the resistance meant that I had to reconcile myself to a long stretch at the Heinkelwerke until a new leadership emerged in the main camp. So my attention turned to where I was and how I might be able to inflict some damage on the Nazi war machine there. The obvious object was the long-range bomber, the He 177. This airplane was beautiful. It was designed to cross the Atlantic and had a range of 6000 kilometres and a payload of over two thousand kilogrammes. Its design was the standard of the time - an aluminum alloy framework covered by shaped aluminum sheets. Self-tightening aluminum alloy rivets held the sheets together and on the frame. My Kommando was responsible for drilling the holes for the rivets and riveting the sheets together. There seemed to be an opportunity here for sabotage, but it depended on my fellow prisoners.

My Polish colleagues were clearly hostile to the Nazis, as were the French, and both groups were willing to fight back. So were the Russians, Ukrainians and Yugoslavs. In fact, many were already engaged in sabotage. Various groups of them were responsible for the plane's subsystems. The Russians took care of the navigational systems. At that time, several of the navigational instruments, like the compass, contained ethyl alcohol which would not freeze at high altitudes. It had a concentration of seventy-five percent, so very potent, although it tasted very sweet. The Russians either poured it out or drank it (only the Russians could drink this and not get roaring drunk), and replaced it with tap water which, of course, would freeze, but only after the plane was airborne for some time. The Ukrainians found some means of taking care of the engine's lubrication. One very easy way to 'freeze' a piston was to add sugar to the engine's gasoline supply. However, sugar was a difficult thing to obtain in the camps and it could be detected in the gasoline. I do not know what they found as an alternative, but they found something because many of the planes crashed into the sea with engines on fire.

Only the German prisoners were reluctant - they did not support material sabotage. Political sabotage, yes, opposing the National Socialist system, yes. But not the purposeful destruction of the product of human hands - for some reason, they were not sure this was acceptable. And then there were the German political prisoners of the right wing who would have still died for their country, as well as those who were former SS officers. So I still had to be careful. It was difficult for me to decide on an appropriate way to contribute to the sabotage. After several days, I had settled on a means. I decided to undermine the structural strength of the fuselage by undermining the riveting.

The shell of the fuselage was made up of a number of aluminum alloy sheets which overlapped and were 'stitched together' with rivets. A riveted connection was made by inserting a rivet, which is a shaft with a head on one end of it, into a hole made in the two overlapping sheets and hammering flat the other end of the rivet where it protrudes from the sheets, using a pneumatic hammer. The hole has to be slightly larger than the rivet's shaft, in order to get the rivet through the two sheets, but only slightly larger, so that when the other end of the rivet is hammered flat, it could not be pulled back through the hole. When squashed, the rivet gets hot and expands. When the rivet cools after the second head is formed, it gets shorter and pulls the two sheets tight together. This pressure contributes to the strength of the riveted connection.

I could not alter the thickness of the sheets or the diameter of the rivets. These came to our Kommando ready for assembly. However, I could change the diameter of the hole we drilled for the rivets and, in that way, significantly reduce the strength of the connections. When the rivets fit properly, the friction between the two sheets resisted the forces tending to pull the sheets apart and the sheets remained in place. When the rivets did not produce sufficient pressure to hold the two metal sheets together, the sheets would tend to pull apart, shearing off the rivets. The fuselage would literally fall apart. This would not happen, however, until the plane was in flight. For this to work, we simply had to cut the holes one tenth of a millimetre larger. This would be enough to cause the rivet to buckle when under pressure, but would not be noticeable to visual inspection on the ground. The squashed head of the rivet would be large enough to cover up the hole while on the ground. It would take the forces of flight to cause the rivets to fail.

I had my plan, but now had to figure out how to implement it. I knew that there were enough men on my Kommando who would help, but I had to be careful of those who opposed sabotage. I could not tamper with either the drills or the riveting system, that would have been too obvious. And then, the inspiration came! One day, one of the aluminum alloy sheets that was to be riveted to a fuselage had been damaged and could not be used. There was no replacement for the sheet and the supervising technician decided to take a sheet of aluminum that was several times weaker than the aircraft aluminum alloy, cut it to shape and fit it to the fuselage. After it was painted, no one could tell the difference. This clarified my thinking - the Luftwaffe both badly needed the planes, and did not have much by way of extra resources at that time. The quality of the manufacturing was not a priority. Thus, all I had to do was arrange to somehow break the drills of the correct diameter.

The next day, as usual, I began the shift with a short talk to the Kommando. This was when special instructions were usually passed on. This time, in a very serious tone, I emphasized the importance of proper riveting to the structural strength of the plane. I explained what would happen if the rivets buckled because the wrong size of drill was chosen and the hole for the rivet was even just slightly too large. I mentioned that it was practically impossible to detect an incorrectly sized hole once the rivet head had been pounded flat, thus they had to be especially diligent. By the next day, there was a serious shortage of drills - an unusual number had been broken "accidentally". It was, of course, mostly the drills of one diameter, the diameter of the hole for the rivets. I informed the supervising technician and he agreed to our using slightly larger drills for the sake of maintaining production, which we did. After several weeks, it seemed that our technological modifications had gone unnoticed.

Evidently, I was wrong. In the middle of November 1942, at the end of my night shift, I noticed the foreman of the Heinkel Kommando coming in my direction. I knew him well - he was a German political prisoner and well-connected with the now rebuilt resistance in the main camp. Yet, he walked past me as if he didn't recognize me, which surprised me. But as he passed, he whispered, "Jerzy, you have two weeks left."

This was a disaster. Apparently I was under suspicion. He would have received the news through the resistance from one of the prisoners working in the Politische Abteilung - the Political Division, who must have seen a list with my name on it. The situation was urgent, because I knew the Gestapo's methods of interrogation and they were brutal. I feared that I would not be able to resist, but neither could I reveal the names of those who worked with me. I had to do something and immediately.

One alternative open to me was due to a quirk in Nazi labour law and the health policy in the camp. Paradoxically, Nazi labour law was applied to KZ inmates, as well as others. If I had a body temperature of 39 degrees Celsius or higher, or an accident on the factory floor, I would be admitted to the KZ hospital. According to that law, as long as I was in the hospital, I could not be interrogated. I could be killed on a whim as soon as I stepped outside of the hospital, but not while I was a patient in it. I had to get myself into the hospital, quickly. One option was to get pneumonia, which I tried in vain to contract by having a hot shower and then running outside into the cool and wet November weather. It didn't work. I was getting desperate, so I arranged a visit to the main camp, ostensibly to get new glasses, so that I could consult the prisoner physicians in the hospital. They confirmed that the best solution was to break a bone, but the question was which bone. I initially thought of the collarbone, until I found out how it was set. It was an incredibly painful procedure, so I decided against that. I considered breaking a leg, but was told that sometimes it took too long for the leg to heal and many ended up being sent to the gas chambers as a result. The only reasonable solution seemed to be to break an arm. They warned me to protect my elbow and wrist while doing it, because they were easily damaged and if they were, it would be a sure sign that it was not an accident. So I returned to the Heinkelwerke.

For my 'accident' to be unnoticed and therefore accepted as an accident, I wanted to be working on the day shift, when there would be many more prisoners on the shop floor, so I arranged the transfer. My first attempt at breaking my arm was a dismal failure. I had padded my wrist and elbow and tried to use the principal of the lever to break it, but my bones were too soft and they would only bend, not break. I was getting desperate as time was running out, so I enlisted the help of a young Polish prisoner I trusted. A few days later, after several unsuccessful attempts, working together, we managed to break one of the bones in my forearm. The pain was not outrageous, but neither of us expected the loud noise it made. My companion immediately disappeared under the fuselage and I quickly unwrapped my elbow and wrist. Then I went to find the foreman. When I reported that I had had a work accident and my arm was broken, he smiled slightly and ordered me onto a truck carrying prisoners to the main camp. When I got to the hospital, it was with a profound sense of relief. One of my friends took care of my fracture. When I woke up several hours later, my arm had been operated on and set, my arm was in a cast and I was in the surgery ward of the KZ hospital.

This did not solve the problem, however, it only postponed it. My personal file was still at Heinkel and I expected to be interrogated as soon as I left the hospital. Still, in the camp, bones healed slowly and it was the end of January 1943 before I was ready to be released. But I was still facing trouble if that happened, so there was no escaping it, my arm had to be broken again. This was done, the arm was reset and my stay in the hospital was extended by at least another two months. The situation was only resolved when the Heinkelwerke was bombed by the Royal Air Force in the spring of 1943 and the plant badly damaged. Apparently my file was destroyed in the fire. Finally, I could leave the hospital. Richard Adler arranged that I be reassigned to the Baubüro. The Heinkel episode was over.

So Pindera was not acting in a vacuum. Rather, he was part of a much larger, complex and shadowy resistance organisation made up primarily of the political prisoners and led by the old guard of the camp, the German communists, who had been in Sachsenhausen since its inception. They ran the camp with a tight fist, for these men not only ran a resistance movement within the barbed wire confines of the camp, but also administered the camp. In all the concentration camps, the prisoners governed themselves, under SS supervision. In Sachsenhausen, it was the German communists, and thus the resistance, who administered the camp. This put those men in a very special and privileged position. They could do much to alleviate the inhumanity of the camp, as well as work toward their goal of undermining the Nazi regime and the war effort.

With the responsibilities of administering the camp came considerable power. Those who ran the camp had a very real impact on the quality of daily life. For example, the SS allocated a certain amount of food to the camp's kitchens. It was up to the prisoners, i.e. the political prisoners led by the communists in this case, to determine how that food was distributed among the inmates. The situation was the same with medications in the hospital. Only so much medicine was available and the camp's prisoner administration determined how it would be allocated. This was a very efficient solution from the perspective of the SS, who were relieved of the tedium and labour-draining responsibility of daily administration of the camp. As well, if something went wrong, it was the prisoners who would be blamed and would pay the price.

The camp administration worked hard to alleviate the worst excesses of camp life and to provide inmates with the means to survive. They were determined to reduce the mortality rate in the camp. Thus, they were careful in the distribution of food, ensuring it was equitable, even if it remained grossly inadequate. They carefully managed the provision of medical care in the camp, so that those who fell ill were given as much of a chance to recover as possible, and those who were beaten or flogged did not die from untended wounds. The communists and other political prisoners were also determined to protect the helpless in the camp. They were especially concerned about the young boys brought to the camp. These were mostly Polish youths who spoke no German and they were easy prey for the predators in the camp. The communists managed to arrange to have them all placed in one barrack called the Jugendblock and they carefully selected Franz Bobzien, a dedicated communist, as its Blockältester. He ensured that the children were protected from sexual exploitation and also arranged German lessons for them, so that they could better cope in the camp.

One of the most difficult situations facing the prisoner leadership was the influx of Soviet prisoners in 1941, thousands of them. Estimates were that there were eighteen thousand of them in all, brought to Sachsenhausen to die. They were housed in a special part of the camp, crammed into eight barracks. As ordered by Hitler, all political commissars among the prisoners, as well as members of the Communist Party of the Soviet Union, were shot immediately. The rest were starved to death. It was a brutal way to die. Pindera still remembers the cartloads of emaciated corpses being hauled past from that corner of the camp, to be taken to the crematorium. Apparently, Pindera learned later, the communists in the camp had organized bread for the Soviet prisoners, as soon as they had arrived. It was not enough, nor could anyone have believed it would be, but it was a gesture of solidarity and support for the Soviet prisoners in their last days. Some thousand of these prisoners were actually allowed to survive, although they worked under brutal conditions. So the communists continued organizing bread for them. It was called the "Red Ball". Pindera remembers this, even from the depths of his own misery on the Speer Kommandos.

A prisoners' work brigade walked along a field where the Soviet prisoners were collecting potatoes, bent over. Several of us in the brigade were carrying concealed pieces of bread for them. I still remember the eyes of the Soviet soldier when I threw him the piece of bread.

This concern for the helpless also extended to the women working in the camp brothel. The brothel was built for the use of the camp inmates. In fact, the Baubüro was given the task of designing and building the brothel in 1943. Pindera was not assigned the design work, as earlier he had botched the design of a pigsty by failing to consider the sexual life of pigs and so was deemed incapable of designing an effective brothel. He was actually rather relieved. The brothel was staffed with female prisoners. Amost all the nationalities were represented, so that there was a Yugslavian woman for the Yugoslavian prisoners; a French woman for the French men; and so on. There were no Jewish girls, because it would have violated German racial law and sexual contact with a Jewish woman would have meant a death sentence for that man, according to Pindera. Nor were professional prostitutes used. The SS charged admission, with an SS officer sitting at the door, selling tickets. The women were all volunteers, or so the men were told. Pindera could not understand the women's willingness to volunteer, so he constructed an opportunity to find out....

Well, you see in the Baubüro, I had considerable freedom of movement. I could always construct an opportunity to go somewhere under the pretence of checking a structure. And that is what I did, I went to inspect the structural soundness of the brothel. As I walked around the outside of the barrack, a young woman was at a window. She was looking out and saw me. I asked her what her nationality was and it turned out to be Polish, although she could not remember what town she came from. Her name was Pasha and she turned out to be sixteen years old. When I asked her why she had volunteered for this job, she told me, "In the camp, I had no chance of staying alive. It was a matter of a few more weeks. I was always hungry, and beaten, and always in pain. Here, nobody beats me. I have enough to eat." She went on to say, "I am only sixteen years old, I did not want to die before I had a chance to know life." It was obvious to me, and to all the political prisoners, that they would be executed at the end of the war, but they did not realize it, it seemed. And unfortunately, we could do nothing to prevent it or to protect them. However, we did have considerable power among the prisoners and especially the political prisoners. We decided that no political prisoner was to make use of the girls' services. The girls, we had concluded, were fellow prisoners - psychologically broken, perhaps, but fellow prisoners. And we were able to enforce this rule strictly. If someone violated it, we arranged to have them shipped out on a transport, which was certain death. I remember one incident, when one of the older political prisoners (he had been in the camp four years) was discovered to have visited the brothel. We confronted him, and he confessed to having been there, but pleaded that he had not made sexual use of the girl. Nonetheless, we arranged to have him on the next transport.

Among the many ways in which the SS exploited the prisoner population was to use them as janitorial staff in their offices. Prisoners swept floors, emptied garbage cans, dusted, cleaned, did routine maintenance. This gave certain men surprising access to the inner sanctums of the SS and thus to an incredible wealth of information that was lying about the offices on desks, thrown out in the garbage, or gleaned from conversations overheard. This was one of the greatest strengths of the resistance in the camp, its ability to gather information. It was made easier by the fact that the prisoner janitors and cleaners were effectively invisible, ignored by the SS officers around whom they worked unobtrusively, much like the way in which staff in an English manor house were trained to be as inconspicuous as possible while they did their work, rendering themselves invisible to their employers, who had learned to look past them rather than at them. This access was useful in several ways. As already suggested, at least it meant that it was possible to warn someone if their name was on a list of prisoners to be interrogated or shipped out on a transport, in the way that Pindera was warned in 1942 when at the Heinkelwerke. It was also possible to manipulate these lists, although it was a very risky thing to do. It was possible to add someone to a list, by substituting the name for another, or to remove someone from a list, by substituting someone else's name for theirs. In this way, the resistance could protect their own and punish transgressors.

In 1944, we discovered that the SS knew about our resistance organisation. You remember that it had already been destroyed once, while I was at the Heinkel factory, but it had been rebuilt. Well, the Gestapo had information about the new organisation. We were warned by prisoners working in the Gestapo and SS offices. The Gestapo had been gathering information for a while and were ready to take action. Apparently, however, they were worried about sparking a camp-wide rebellion if they swept in and arrested everyone, so they had decided to arrest people a few at a time. They had a list and one of our spies had seen it at the Inspektionskoncentrationslager - the Concentration Camp Inspection office. My name was on it, I was told. Colleagues were trying to take counter-measures, but the situation was grave. The SS fell into a pattern, which was a nerve-wracking one for all involved. Between one and three o'clock in the morning, three SS officers would enter a selected barrack, quietly awaken the Blockältester and ask him to guide them to the bed of the prisoner to be arrested. He would lead them to the bed, where they would quietly wake the prisoner, ask him his number and name, and order him to stand up and follow them out. I know this because one night, I heard them arrest someone from my block who was sleeping not far from me. Only once did I hear any resistance - it was a night when, rumour had it, they had arrested fifteen men. That particular group must have fought back because we heard a number of shots ring out from not far away. I do not know how many were arrested in total, but the operation lasted about three weeks.

Needless to say, I got very little sleep, as I was waiting for the tap on my shoulder. Of course, I could find time to sleep during the day at the Baubüro. Occasionally, I could sneak into the lumberyard and fall asleep behind or on top of a stack of boards. The problem with that was it would have been easy to oversleep and then I would have been in serious trouble. So I took to sleeping under my desk in the office. It was a huge desk and I could curl up in the kneehole easily. Once, Schnöll came looking for me. He had a question to ask. Of course, I was asleep under my desk and did not dare to crawl out. I would have been in trouble then. So I had to stay in hiding. He sat down at my desk to wait for me and began to examine my drawings and calculations. So I was lying under my desk with his boots inches from my nose, praying he would go away, racking my brain for an acceptable explanation for my situation. It was such an unbelievably stupid and dangerous situation. Eventually Schnöll gave up and left. Later, we all laughed about it, but at the time, I was very frightened.

After a couple of weeks of poor sleep and nightly arrests, I was finally given a reprieve. Someone came to me and told me, "Go, you may sleep quietly. Somebody died and it was your number." They had arranged to exchange my number on the list with someone else's, someone who had died. They took my place. I do not know how many were saved like that.

The political prisoners could also inflict their own punishment on those found to have transgressed the unwritten rules of the camp. A particularly vicious SS officer might be found with gold coins from Kanada in his pocket, a guaranteed death sentence for the officer, either immediate or a prolonged one, served at the Eastern Front or as a camp inmate, as he was clearly guilty of corruption. As already seen, a political prisoner who violated the interdiction to visit the brothel could be dealt with summarily by assigning them to a transport. Something similar might have happened to someone who stole another's bread, at least in the early years, when to do so was considered tantamount to murdering a fellow prisoner. But the most spectacular example of prisoners' justice was the execution of a fellow prisoner, known as Staniczek. Pindera was not in the camp that day, but heard what happened when he returned that evening.

Staniczek was the most infamous killer among the prisoners. It was said that he had personally killed over 345 of his fellow prisoners, in particularly brutal and horrific ways, and often on his own initiative, without being ordered to kill by the SS. Staniczek was a political prisoner, but the only one I knew who killed. In addition, he was a communist, which was both a major embarrassment for the communist leadership in the camp, and an enormous shame. He was from Silesia, and spoke German and the old Polish dialect of that region. I had had to work with him once, when building the barbed wire fence around the Klinkenwerk satellite camp. I had particularly bitter feelings about that Kommando, because I was building a cage for myself and fellow prisoners. He did not harm me, but I did not like him. Staniczek was now being moved from the Klinkenwerk camp back to the main camp. He had been assigned to his old block in the main camp and he arrived at the camp at noon on that Saturday. Word spread through the camp instantly, "Staniczek is back." The Blockältester showed him his place at the table, gave him a bowl, spoon and fork, and assigned him space in a locker. Each time, the Blockältester told Staniczek the name of the prisoner who had used that seat, bowl, fork, locker before him. They were all prisoners he had killed. When Staniczek put his things in the locker, the other prisoners removed their belongings. When he sat down at the table, all the other prisoners left the table and ate their meal while standing. When he asked a question, no one answered. That evening, three of the oldest political prisoners presented Staniczek with a bouquet of roses, held together by a long rope. There was a note attached that read, "For personal use. Please hurry." Staniczek was never insulted, never spoken to harshly. In fact, he was never spoken to at all, or even acknowledged as present. He was treated as if he simply did not exist. He was a perfect non-person.

On Sunday morning, after I had left the camp, several hundred political prisoners gathered outside of Staniczek's barrack. They shouted epithets at him, cursed him, told him to go to the devil. By mid-morning, Staniczek apparently made up his mind. He asked everyone to leave the room, announcing he was going to hang himself. When the crowd heard that, it became rowdier. As I heard it, three times Staniczek mounted the stool and three times he stepped down. The crowd was derisive. "You coward! You are brave only when you murder!" The fourth time, Staniczek kicked away the stool. In this manner, the political prisoners cleared their ranks of the corrupt.

Such punishment was not just reserved for fellow prisoners. The political prisoners were also able to touch even some of the most powerful SS officers. One was Oswald Pohl. Pohl was Himmler's administrative chief, responsible for running the SS economic empire under the auspices of the SS-Central Administrative and Economic Office (SS-HAVW). Thus, Pohl was one of the most important men in the SS.

As I remember Oswald Pohl, he was an efficient and talented administrator and totally ruthless in his treatment of the KZ prisoners. He never raised his voice and his manners were always correct, but he was always very cool towards the prisoners. As far as he was concerned, we did not exist for him as human beings. We were only just tolerated as a source of labour and so were permitted to live only as long as we were needed. He had a dog, a German Shepherd, which he had trained to despise prisoners and to kill on command, much like the dogs of the SS Death's Head Division, used to hunt and kill prisoners. Pohl often came to the Baubüro, together with his dog, so we knew of him. He was tall, well-built, elegantly dressed and with an expressionless face. I myself had spoken with Pohl twice, once to report my presence at the construction site of the Heart's Ace, and once about the design for an air-raid shelter at his private residence in a village close to Oranienburg. That meant I had to visit his home. His wife was as disdainful of prisoners as her husband. Pohl was held in low esteem among the prisoners. He was not hated, as he had done nothing to deserve our hatred, but he was despised. Although we could not touch Pohl directly, an opportunity arose to touch him indirectly. One day, when he was visiting the Baubüro, he left his dog in the antechamber as usual. I told Paul, the political prisoner who ran the scrap metal recycling shop, that the dog was in the foyer. Paul came by the office, asking an innocent question. He had a long piece of twine with him, and a piece of sausage or some such meat tied to the end. He used that to lure the dog out of the antechamber, then he killed it. He used the cauldron in the shop to make a stew from the dog's carcass. There was enough so that everyone in the Baubüro got a bowl. I remember having the pleasure of watching Pohl through a window as he talked to Schnöll while I and the other prisoners ate his dog. When Pohl went to leave, of course, he couldn't find the animal. The prisoners at the camp gate all swore they saw it run through the gate.

Part Four

Death March

It was April 1945. The Soviet Army was advancing on Berlin and the Americans were approaching from the West. At night, the prisoners in Sachsenhausen could hear the heavy thunder of the Soviet artillery and, during the day, they could watch the Soviet fighter planes chasing the overpowered German planes. The first changes at the camp were ones that few noticed. The brothel was shut down, the women gone. No one saw them leave the camp, but suddenly they were no longer there. At the same time, Pindera believes that the Falschwerkstatt was also shut down and its Kommando of prisoners exterminated as well. The atmosphere was very tense in the camp, as no one knew what the SS would do with the prisoners. Matters were not helped by the fact that the political prisoners' source of information had been cut off. The last reliable news from the Concentration Camp Inspection Office was received mid-April. They had heard that the Soviet Army had crossed the river Oder and was moving in the direction of Berlin, crushing all opposition in its path. At that point, the janitorial services provided by Sachsenhausen to the SS adminstrative offices had been abruptly cancelled and that invaluable information source had died.

What made the matter worse was that we could no longer learn about the plans made for our future. We knew that an order from Himmler to kill all prisoners in the camps had been rescinded for technical reasons, but we did not know what was being planned as an alternative. Strangely, it was the older prisoners who were the most tense. It seemed that the youth firmly believed the end of the war would bring liberation and could not believe that the SS might consider exterminating them in one last, mad slaughter.

Refugee prisoners - men, women and children - were flooding into Sachsenhausen from camps further east that were being overrun by the Soviets. Rather than leaving the prisoners to be liberated by the USSR, the SS brought the prisoners with them as the German forces retreated before the Soviet onslaught. The population of the camp exploded, reaching over 95,000 by March 1945. The camp's prisoner administration was not unduly thrown by the influx of population, other than the presence of so many women in the camp for the first time. It proved a serious challenge to try to control the male population, who had not seen women sometimes for years.

Pindera can only remember once when discipline broke...

We were outside the main camp, at the *Bauleitung der Waffen-SS und Polizei*. Early that afternoon, the air raid sirens went off and we could hear the roar of bombs bursting around us. The SS guards raced for the air raid shelter, ordering us to do the same. Ignoring them, we climbed to the roof of the building to watch the attack. We felt invulnerable! I remember watching a house close to us. A bomb had hit it and the whole house lifted in the air and then disintegrated. We didn't feel sorry for the people of the city. They lived right beside the camp and had to have known what was happening there and yet did nothing. Amazingly, when the air raid was over, we were not punished for our insubordination.

Then word was passed that the camp was to be evacuated. This was soon followed by official orders. The evacuation began on 21 April. The prisoners were to be sorted by nationality and then marched out of the camp in columns five wide, in groups of 500. The first prisoners to leave were given some food to take with them - a loaf of bread and 250 grams of sausage - but those supplies soon ran out and the last prisoners to leave received nothing.

As I did not know what the evacuation procedure would be, or whether we would be searched when leaving the camp, I did not arrange for any food supplies. I did, however, organize my clothing. I got hold of a pair of good, strong, comfortable shoes out of *Kanada*, as well as new clothes - civilian clothes, rather than our striped uniforms. This was less a problem than you might suspect, because the usual uniform was in short supply by this point. As long as the clothes were marked according to the camp dress code, I could wear anything. This meant that the clothes had to have stripes on them, painted on with a red oil-based paint. You also had to have a large red cross painted on the back of the jacket and a red square attached to the jacket, above the cross. I arranged that my new clothes' stripes would be done with a water-based paint that could be washed out and that the red square could be easily removed. I also made a small bag in which I could carry my notebook, letters, a pocket knife, some needles and thread, and the addresses of my closest friends. I also carried a shoulder bag for a spare shirt, underwear and socks, as well as a shaving razor, toothbrush, toothpaste and soap. Finally, I had a water canteen and a thin cotton blanket. I was as ready as I was going to be.

On 20 April, Hitler's birthday, we were ordered to stay in the camp. For the first time since I had arrived at Sachsenhausen, there were no roll calls in the *Appellplatz*. We were informed that, the next day, the KZ would be evacuated. All the prisoners - men, women and children - who were able to move on foot would leave the camp in columns of five hundred. The sick would remain in the camp's hospital barracks. There would be no provision made for the transportation of weak prisoners. Prisoners would either keep up with their columns or be shot. At least now we knew what we could expect.

Discipline in the camp was starting to break down. The old political prisoners, including myself, were still behaving, and we tried to maintain order in the camp. That proved very difficult. Some prisoners were using this opportunity to seek revenge and settle accounts. Meanwhile, the roar of the Soviet artillery was now continuous. The next morning, the evacuation began. There was no inspection at the main gate and little control over who joined which column. People joined whichever one they wished. The women's columns left first. Then came the various nationalities.

I had hung back. I wanted to wait until it was clear that the prisoners leaving the KZ were not being executed just outside. This precaution was a mistake. The first columns received food packets that were sufficient for several days. But by the time my column passed through the gate, they were handing out only bread. The older prisoners carefully divided the bread into five portions, so it would last five days. We expected to spend the nights in barns and thought we would be able to find some rye or wheat we could cook into a kind of porridge, if we were lucky. So we brought along small steel cans to boil the grain if the opportunity arose.

The first afternoon was uneventful. As expected, the younger prisoners were unable to control their hunger and ate much of their bread ration immediately. We could not have been able to stop them, even if we had tried - besides, talking was strongly discouraged and these men knew the dangers. If they chose to ignore the advice, we could do nothing for them. That night we spent in a barn. It was, relatively speaking, comfortable - it was warm and dry, there was some straw to sleep on. I slept well. However, others did not fare so well. Those who had eaten too much bread found themselves with severe cramps and diarrhea. By morning, they were in such trouble that they were unable to march and so were summarily shot. And so began the fatalities.

The next day, 22 April, was a difficult one. Many prisoners were not used to this much walking and their shoes were inadequate. This made it very difficult for them to keep up with the column. Our particular SS guard did not seem keen to completely exterminate his column and so, every two or three hours, he allowed us to rest for ten minutes. If he could, he would try to take the break near a village well, so we could quench our thirst. The pace was not gruelling - maybe about three or four kilometres per hour. Yet, corpses started to appear along the side of the road. Sometimes someone would simply collapse. Other times, an individual would give up, step out of the column, cross the ditch and sit down, waiting for a gunshot to the neck.

The third day, the misery mounted. The numbers of prisoners executed along the sides of the road and even in village streets, increased quickly. In the morning, it seemed there was a corpse every 100 metres. By the afternoon, it seemed that they were every five or ten metres. And in the afternoon, we saw the first corpses of women and children. Interestingly, we had been unmoved by the men who had died at the side of the road. After years in the camp, where we had watched thousands of men die, literally, in every conceivable way, we had become hardened to that kind of death. But to see women and children dead at the side of the road shocked us. Women carry life. Women are special. Women should never die in a ditch. The execution of women was obscene to us, still. And to kill children! Children were also very special, something to be cherished and protected and nurtured. To harm a child was to attack the family, the home, to attack innocence. It shook us badly.

As usual, no food was supplied, only water. However, we were allowed to gather up kernels of rye and wheat when we had reached that evening's destination. The atmosphere was somber, as the numbers of the dead had mounted over the course of the day. The fourth day of the evacuation was a very difficult one. This was the day on which everyone's food ran out, even those who had carefully apportioned the food they had received when setting out from the camp. And the number of prisoners shot and dying in the ditches was increasing. I still had one small portion of bread for the next day, but I could not imagine how I would survive afterwards. Then the SS officer in charge of our column did something unimaginable - he bought some potatoes from a farmer, had them cooked in their skins, and distributed them among the prisoners. I got three of them, and they tasted delicious. Still, we felt alone and abandoned, surrounded by grim SS guards, glared at by the occasional hostile farmer we passed, a grey sky overhead. No sign of help, of compassion, of friendliness. And no trace of the American forces, not even an airplane. It seemed that they did not care.

However, we had underestimated the bravery and dedication of the Red Cross. The Red Cross got permission from Heinrich Himmler to follow the evacuation marches with ambulances and food. I never saw them in action, but my friends did, and they told me what the Red Cross did. The Red Cross followed closely on the heels of the columns, in spite of the threats of the SS guards, and the young Red Cross volunteers were ready to spring from their vehicles in a split second. Because they rode high in their buses, they could see over the column ahead of them, and when they noticed a prisoner leaving the column, they jumped down with a stretcher and ran as fast as they could to reach him before the SS could dispatch him with a shot in the neck. They were mostly successful, although there were not nearly enough ambulances. At the end of the day, the Red Cross representative would request permission to distribute food to the prisoners. Although my column was not so lucky, just the fact that someone was trying to help raised our spirits enormously. Yet still there was no sign of the Allies.

For several days we were practically without food and our SS guard stopped giving us breaks during the day. We were all reduced to something like automotons, concentrating on putting one foot in front of the other. That day, two things happened that challenged me, and found me wanting, at least in my own eyes. The first incident was a simple one, but one for which I still feel shame. I was marching in my column, when I felt someone touch my arm, and softly ask, "Water." My first instinct was to unhook my canteen and pass it over. But then I glanced at the person asking for help. I was stunned. Although he was difficult to recognize (the march had changed him), he was well-known in the camp. It was Kokosinski. He was notorious in the camp, and had been the uncrowned king of the KZ for the past few months because of his open collaboration with the SS. He had a reputation for causing the deaths of a number of fellow prisoners. He was the last who should have needed help, because of his connections. He was the last who deserved help. I turned away and kept my canteen to myself. Now, many years later, my feelings are more ambivalent. I had broken a cardinal rule among the political prisoners - always help your fellow prisoner, even if it might endanger your life.

That same day, I was faced with another, even more momentous decision, and again I bitterly regret the choice I made. The roadside had been strewn with corpses all day and I was emotionally exhausted. As we marched along, I saw a young man step out of his place near the middle of my column - I was near the rear - and cross to the ditch where he sat down. He was clearly waiting to be executed. I could see the SS guard had noticed him, and he was already taking his gun from his shoulder in order to kill him. I had about ten seconds to make my decision. It would have been just possible to step out of the column, put the young man on my back, and step back into the column. I could have carried the boy for a few kilometres before making appropriate arrangements. But the guard was already alerted and he might have shot both of us. We could have triggered a general panic. And I wanted to live. We had heard, in the last days in the camp, that the Soviet Union had 'liberated' Poland. My Polish colleagues and I had decided that, when we were free, we would return to Poland to try to lessen the impact of the communist takeover and contribute to Poland's recovery. And so I froze, unable to make a decision. The seconds slipped by. And then I heard a shot. It was over, and I had failed. It is a decision that has haunted me the rest of my life.

Later that day, perhaps in order to make up for my indecision and cowardice earlier, when another prisoner stepped from the column, several of us moved decisively to prevent him. He was an old prisoner, a scion of an old Polish family. Despair had engulfed him and he wished to die. We, his friends, goaded him to make him angry. It was a lesson we had learned in the camp, to get a man so angry that he would march to hell on broken legs in order to kill the devils. And we did this, even using our fists to do it. Our methods were shameful, our goal was not. And we succeeded, because he survived.

After eight days of marching, I had had enough, as had some of my colleagues. We decided to escape. That morning, we cleaned ourselves as best we could, and shaved. I had washed the red stripes out of my clothes the night before. Before we moved out in our columns, some friends of ours created a diversion in a corner of the barn in which we had stayed the night before. While there was commotion, I and my two friends slipped out through a hole in the back of the barn and jumped the fence. We headed for the forest, which was close by. The first 200 metres were very difficult, I had such an unpleasant feeling on my back! We had to walk across the field, not run, as if we were farm help going to work. It was incredibly difficult to walk slowly. When we got close to the forest, the youngest of us, Stefan, could not bear it anymore and he jumped over the ditch and ran for cover. That meant we had no choice, we had to do the same. And, of course, this caught the attention of the guards, who began to chase us. And then other prisoners took advantage of the guards' departure to escape to the forest themselves, so the result was a general hunt for prisoners in the forest.

The situation was very dangerous. We had to hide. I found a large spruce tree, and its lower branches formed a canopy that swept the ground. I told my friends to crawl under there, because no one would see us. This is what we did, and we lay there with our heads on the ground, watching out from under the tree. Suddenly we could see boots, coming in our direction. Then the boots stopped and turned. They started to move away. Then they stopped again. Stefan could not stand it. And he crawled out from under the tree, and began to run. Of course, he got caught. I heard the SS guard ask him, "Are you a prisoner from the camp?", to which he replied, "Yes." "Are you alone?" "No." "Where are your comrades?" He said, "There." I could not see, but he must have pointed. I was sure he had given us away. But then we saw the boots disappear quickly in another direction! He had pointed away from us! So we waited about ten minutes and then crawled out from under the tree. We began to work our way through the forest. At one point, we came to an open firebreak in the forest and, three hundred yards up the way, we saw Stefan with the guard. But we were too far away and we dashed across the fire break and to freedom. The next day, Stefan joined us! That night, the prisoners had been put in a barn, and several of them had simply dug out under the foundation and got away.

Amazingly, within three hours of his escape, Pindera wrote a letter to his mother. He had no idea how it would get to her, but it was perhaps a very personal gesture of defiance and determination...

Dear Mother,
I enclose your last letter - I am writing this 'on the fly'. We were evacuated and after 8 days, we have had it up to here, enough of this. I am, together with two of my colleagues, taking a chance. I am writing these words in the forest three hours after our escape. We will try, using all means, to go to the front line *(their intention was to somehow cross the German eastern front line and get back to Poland)*. We

hope that we will be happy. So, Mama, chin up. We will
meet after the war. I send hugs and kisses to you and Dani.

*The next day, Pindera reported, he spent the whole day sitting in
the sun and eating strawberry preserves from a small jar using a silver
teaspoon which he had taken from an abandoned mansion. Two days
later, the Red Army arrived. That day, he drank good French brandy
with two young Soviet officers, in celebration of the defeat of the Nazis.
Pindera eventually returned to Poland, although he stopped at
Sachsenhausen for a short while to regain his strength. He stayed there
about one week, before setting out for home. For him, the war against
the Germans was finally over.*

Epilogue

The war may have been over, but like so many others, Pindera would grapple with the consequences, physical and emotional, of his internment for many, many years. It had been a searing experience, and one whose lessons he mulled over for a long time. It would have been easy to slide into simple, blind hatred, but his experiences made this unacceptable to him. As he wrote...

I expected that during the first several years after the war there would be a huge amount of hatred. Justified hatred, yes, but hatred leads nowhere. It would be necessary to build bridges over painful memories.

He argued that it was important to remember that the Germans, and even the SS, were not "homogeneously bad", just as the camp inmates were not homogeneously good. He had had enough encounters with SS who proved honourable and even humane, and with prisoners who were brutal and inhumane, to understand this. Perhaps the most outstanding example of an honourable SS officer was Bauleiter SS Obersturmführer Josef Schnöll. In several instances, Schnöll should have severely punished prisoners in the Baubüro, but chose to turn a blind eye. In one instance, Pindera should have been condemned to a nasty death - when he had refused to submit a report to Schnöll about the state of the Kino construction site that would have condemned the foreman and prisoners to certain death. Too many times, Schnöll found a way to avoid inflicting punishment or seeing punishable activities. In Pindera's words, Josef Schnöll was an exceptional man deserving high respect. In a letter to Schnöll's family sent long after the war was over, Pindera wrote...

129

Starting from February 1942 I was assigned to work in the design office, Baubüro der Bauleitung der Waffen SS und Polizei. To my recollection, during the time when the head of the Baubüro was Obersturmführer Josef Schnöll, the Baubüro was a kind of oasis of humanity where, during the work hours, the prisoners were treated strictly but properly, as prisoners of war. This was very exceptional in the concentration camps where the commanding SS officers were promoting inhumanity, as a rule. I feel strongly that it is my moral duty to state that, to my knowledge, the behaviour of SS Obersturmführer Josef Schnöll was always correct and deserving respect... I deeply regret that Josef Schnöll passed away before I could tell him in person how highly I esteemed his conduct as a man and as a human being, how often I remembered his exemplary conduct during all the years which passed since that time, and how much I appreciated and valued his understanding of my attitude.

Schnöll was not the only German who earned Pindera's respect and gratitude. When recounting today the story of the little girl with the green apples, risking everything to get food to the prisoners working on the sewers in Oranienburg, he was still awed at her mother's and the girl's bravery. So, he refused to fall into what he considered the trap of condemning all Germans as uniformly bad. Still, Pindera also did not forgive those who did not deserve it. He was impatient with other SS officers who, on the surface, might have made claims for the same respect. One such man was the head of the crematorium.

He was a rather tall man, strongly built, with a pleasant face. His manners were correct. He spoke in a quiet voice, without raising it, as was common among the Blockführers, and he never killed nor even hit a prisoner in anger. I was told that personally he was quite a decent man who very often expressed his compassion for the prisoners and his sympathy with their fate, and supported his words with deeds: a forgotten sandwich left in places accessible to prisoners; an unlit cigarette absentmindedly thrown away; not noticing the illegal pieces of clothing which prisoners wore to keep warm; short, pleasant conversations with prisoners; and so on. A very decent man in the uniform of an SS officer, who even bent the law a bit to help unfortunate prisoners - as long as it did not violate his principles or his notion of duty. Nonetheless, he continued to run the crematorium. He had accepted totally the Nazi sense of duty, but nevertheless was able to maintain his own, private realm of moral decency all the while carrying out the tasks assigned him - an SS officer who managed to make incompatibles compatible, at least in his own conscience. He performed his job as humanely as possible, dispatching prisoners cleanly, efficiently, quickly, without prolonging the agony.

While Pindera respected the man's professionalism and the respectful manner in which he dispatched prisoners, he ultimately dismissed this man as "subjectively decent" but essentially amoral, a warning for future generations, rather than a role model. He argued that this man had set aside moral principles and the notion of personal honour in favour of an absolute sense of duty, which was a trap and a betrayal of all that is civilized. He had a similar lack of patience for a group of three young SS officers who approached him in the weeks just before the death march...

"Herr Pindera, we would like to talk with you." Three young Bauführers stopped me in the entrance hall to the Baubüro. Nobody was around, we were alone. I was shocked, and not a little afraid. It was not good to get singled out like this. Being addressed as "Herr" was also not a good sign. Such an opening sentence generally was a precursor to a long and painful interrogation. It was the last days of March 1945, when the situation in the camp was already tense. We all knew that the Soviet Army was sweeping westward and that the war was already lost for the Reich. It was also uncertain whether Himmler wanted all the camp inmates executed or not, so the prisoners were very apprehensive and cautious. I was afraid that these men had uncovered my resistance activities and were here to punish me. It seemed particularly ironic and stupid that I should be killed just on the eve of liberation. The most important thing for me was to maintain my dignity, so I looked the officers in the face and replied very formally, "I am at your disposal."

Another spoke, then, and left me completely astonished. "We want you to know why we did what we did and that we recognize our transgressions." I was pleased to hear them say this. If nothing else, it meant that the morale and cohesion of the SS was finally breaking down, but I still feared why they had chosen to tell me, in particular, this. I could only guess it was because they knew I was connected to the camp's resistance. But, as they were making this confession to me, it seemed that they would not likely act on that suspicion. Still, one had to be careful.

What they then told me clarified, in my mind, the apparent inconsistencies I had observed in the behaviour of various SS officers over the years of imprisonment. I was still shocked by what they had to say. At that time, I was deeply imbued with the notions of honour and motherland, and that nothing was as important as protecting both. These officers explained the particular notion of duty toward their own nation that they had been taught, a notion that required that duty override all ethical standards that might have stood in the way. One explained, "We wish you to know that we are now aware that we have been deceived. We were told that we were going to be heroes, but it turned out that we became like criminals." I did not dare to say anything, so I only indicated that I was listening. He went on to explain that, after their stint in the Hitler Youth, they received further political and leadership education at a special school. I knew of these institutions - there, the students are taught blind devotion, that an order of a leader overrides all ethical, moral and legal principles, systems or standards. It was considered the most honourable thing to follow an order of a superior. Loyalty was honour. The young officer continued, that at the time of graduation, they were called to the office of the school's commandant, and asked a number of very personal questions, including their level of patriotism. In particular, they were asked whether they were ready to carry out, without reservation, any task that was necessary to ensure the future of the German nation. They were young and patriotic, so they answered affirmatively. Having been assured of their commitment, the commandant became more specific. He said that there were tasks needed doing that fell outside the principles of the bourgeois capitalist morality that had prevailed before the Reich. Because of the importance of these tasks, which would be remembered for centuries, only certain special men could perform them. They would be difficult and unpleasant tasks, and only men of the highest ethical level could succeed. But they would have to suppress their ethical principles, isolate themselves from what they had learned from their parents and teachers, and they would have to sacrifice themselves for the sake of the Fatherland. Their individual deeds and individual sacrifices might be forgotten, but the results of their actions would allow the German nation to rule the world. Such were the words of the commandant.

The spokesman for the three officers told me that they felt chosen and honoured. They were young and inexperienced, and believed in the importance of their heroic task, which they accepted. Much later, they became too familiar with the reality of the concentration camps and with political prisoners. And they began to have doubts. They gradually ceased to consider themselves heroes. What occurred before their eyes was not honourable. In the end, they had concluded that they had been deceived; that they were not heroes, but villains. And that the acts they committed were dishonourable, unethical and criminal. They concluded by suggesting, jokingly, that perhaps we would meet again in Warsaw, but in reversed roles - with them performing the manual work to rebuild the destroyed city - as punishment for their crimes. They then left me, without me offering the prescribed formula when leaving the presence of an SS officer. I had no doubt that those officers were both open and sincere. The bitterness they felt at being deceived was clear. Still, I could not and cannot forgive them. They had violated basic moral standards, the honour that is based upon those standards and had participated in unspeakable crimes.

Pindera went on to write that the lesson to be drawn from this incident was about the great power of deception. These young men had committed heinous crimes and, having done so, earned his deep disgust, but Pindera reserved his greater disgust for those who deceived these young men into believing that what they were doing was honourable. The greater enemy was not the deceived, but the one deceiving, those who had taught these young men to abandon basic moral values.

It was not just the SS who posed such complex moral problems. The prisoner population itself, in all its complexity, exhibited a whole spectrum of responses to the circumstances in which it found itself.

Some prisoners were only concerned about their own survival, while others were also concerned about the survival of others. Still others chose to fight back, as well as survive. So it is a mistake to consider the camp inmates as passive victims. It is important to realize that not all prisoners were the same, that there were factions within the camp population, not all of whom agreed. There were several categories into which prisoners sorted themselves - political, asocial, criminal, homosexual, religious fundamentalists, and so on. These factions seldom intermingled. The prisoners were also divided and marked according to their national origin: German, Polish, French, Ukrainian, and so on. Each of these groups had their own priorities, which might not have always meshed with those of other groups. And each acted according to their own needs and interests. In fact, there was often stiff fighting internally, between factions, and especially between the political prisoners on one hand, and the criminal prisoners on the other. This was especially true because the criminal element did not share the political prisoners' determination to fight Nazism.

And, as seen in the example of Staniczek, being a prisoner did not make a person sympathetic towards other prisoners. There were cruel and inhumane prisoners, as well as Germans. What allowed this cruelty and inhumanity to flourish was the particularly vicious and carefully calculated camp system constructed by the Nazis. This system purposefully cultivated such people and gave them free rein to exercise their sadism, for the system's ultimate purpose was to break the prisoners physically and spiritually, to rob them of their dignity, honour and soul - those things that are the best of what it is to be human. That was its logic. Survival, in such an environment, was an enormously difficult and all-consuming task. Some, like Pindera, found the means to survive; too many others did not.

Pindera felt it important to understand why so many broke under the weight of this system of terror, while others did not. Those who succumbed to the terror were usually good and decent people, Pindera observed, who were both completely unprepared for the hell into which they had been thrown and incapable of understanding its purpose. This left them exceedingly vulnerable, because they were confused, helpless and mentally paralyzed by the unspeakable cruelty surrounding them. They were mentally lost, as they could not perceive the system and so could not understand it. Without understanding it, one could not survive it. So, according to Jerzy Pindera, a key to surviving the camps was to understand the reasons and logic underlying the system of terror imposed. Knowledge was power. Understanding the system made it possible for a prisoner to start to fight back, by resisting the terror.

But survival was more than just understanding the system. If the essence of that system was about breaking the prisoners, not just physically, but even more so, emotionally and spiritually, then, argued Pindera, the key to survival was the strength of one's character. In order to survive, mentally and spiritually as much as physically, one had to cleave hard to one's principles, moral standards and sense of honour - to preserve, as best one can, in every gesture and action, those things the Nazis were determined to destroy - one's dignity, honour, strength of character.

This, Pindera argued, was not as impossible to do as you might think, once a key realisation was made. Once you acknowledged that you could die at any moment and that you had really no control over when or whether it happened, and once you had come to terms with this realisation, decisions were made much easier. Pindera soon came to recognize that, while he did not want to die, he could die easily, and that the odds were very good that he would die before getting out of the camp. He found that once he had recognized and accepted this, it became easier for him to fight back, for he no longer feared dying. It made his choices much simpler, because they were not muddied by concerns about self-preservation. This also made it much easier for him to hold hard to his principles and dignity. Since his life was always at risk, as he could be killed on a guard's whim at any moment or for any number of often inane reasons, decisions were not made based on the risks they posed to his life, but whether it was the right thing to do or not, whether it advanced the fight against the Nazis or not, whether it protected or endangered other prisoners or not. For Pindera, the crucial thing that marked a survivor was the strength of their character, their strong sense of moral principle and of personal dignity. Without honour or personal dignity, one was lost. It was this realisation that carried him through his years in the camps and shaped the remainder of his life. It was this realisation that resulted in his dismissal of the SS as base traitors to civilisation, by permitting themselves to compromise their morals and to sacrifice what was right and good. Excuses for such compromises were not acceptable. In the end, one's principles, one's character were all that one had, and all that one has. Without them, an individual was lost.

Index